ONE POT
FEEDS ALL

DARINA ALLEN
ONE POT
FEEDS ALL

100 new one-dish recipes
from roasts to desserts

Photography by Lizzie Mayson

Kyle Books

An Hachette UK Company
www.hachette.co.uk

First published in Great Britain in 2019 by
Kyle Books, an imprint of Kyle Cathie Ltd
Carmelite House
50 Victoria Embankment
London EC4Y 0DZ
www.kylebooks.co.uk

This edition published in 2020

ISBN: 978 0 85783 713 4

Distributed in the US by Hachette Book Group, 1290
Avenue of the Americas, 4th and 5th Floors, New
York, NY 10104

Distributed in Canada by Canadian Manda Group,
664 Annette St., Toronto, Ontario, Canada M6S 2C8

Printed and bound in China

10 9 8 7 6 5 4 3 2 1

Dedication
For all the heroic young
couples who are trying to
keep all the balls in the air.

Publisher **JOANNA COPESTICK**
Editor **VICKY ORCHARD**
Editorial assistant **SARAH KYLE**
Design **HELEN BRATBY**
Photography **LIZZIE MAYSON***
Food styling **ANNIE RIGG**
Props styling **LINDA BERLIN**
Production **GEMMA JOHN**

*Excludes portrait on page 6 © Peter Cassidy

Contents

INTRODUCTION

One pot, one dish, one roasting pan, I can't believe it's taken me so long to write this book as it's been bubbling away in my subconscious for years. It is over a decade since we added a One-Pot Wonders course to our schedule at the Ballymaloe Cookery School. From the word go it was a big hit and its enduring popularity is a sure sign that this way of cooking is here to stay.

This book is for all of you who really want to cook delicious, wholesome food for yourselves and those you love, but find it virtually impossible to keep all the balls in the air, battling home through rush hour traffic, dashing into the store to grab some ingredients, and then doing your best to cook from scratch, in full knowledge that beautiful freshly cooked produce has the best flavor and is super nutritious. For growing numbers of people, it's simply not possible,

yet I can still hear my mother's words ringing in my ears: "If you don't get wholesome, nourishing, delicious food onto the table to keep the family healthy, happy, and bouncing with energy, you'll give the money to the doctor or the chemist." But what to do?

Well, hopefully this book will provide some solutions. I've collected my favorite one-pot dishes; some time-honored favorites honed over the years, others developed more recently when we were testing recipes specifically for this book. Because my brief was that everything had to be cooked in one pot, against my better judgement, I experimented with some one-pot pasta dishes with great success. By increasing the liquid in some other dishes, I discovered that I could add rice, pearl barley, orzo, and beans to the various

pots with delicious results—so you really can get your whole meal from one dish. Of course, you can still cook them separately, if you like, but believe me this one-pot method works brilliantly.

It's not just pots and pans—my roasting pans and baking sheets are in constant use. I love to layer up gratins and to roast fish and meat over vegetables, or just roast a selection of vegetables with lots of gutsy herbs and olive oil.

Some recipes, such as Lamb & Pearl Barley Stew (page 74), are naturally one-pot dishes, with chunks of sweet lamb, carrots, onions, a sprig of thyme. But there are plenty more examples.

Many of these one-pot recipes reheat brilliantly, or can be frozen in portions to make your life easier on another occasion, such as the Super-easy Chicken Casserole (page 57), Chili con Carne (page 65), Cod, Hake, or Haddock with Dill and Pangratatto (page 101), Venison & Parsnip Stew (page 85), Lamb, Butternut Squash & Orzo Stew (page 76) or the Black-eyed Pea, Pumpkin & Chickpea Stew (page 124).

So, what's not to love about one-pot, one-dish, or one-roasting-pan cooking? For a start, there's less washing up. It's a brilliant option if you don't have much time and there's no longer any need to feel guilt-ridden. With the recipes in this book, you simply pop everything into the pot, add some herbs and spices, bring to a boil, cover, and put into the oven or simmer on the stovetop while you catch up with other chores, help with homework, or just put your feet up and enjoy a well-deserved cup of tea or glass of wine. This way of cooking is also perfect for easy entertaining—who doesn't love a juicy stew or casserole? Ladle it out at the table directly from the pot and follow it with a salad of organic leaves for a perfect meal.

An electric slow cooker or Crock-Pot is also worth considering as part of your kitchen kit, perfect for slow cooking and gentle braises and of course for making stock.

Pots, pans, and sheets

You don't need much in the way of kitchen kit, but it's good to invest in a few sturdy pans and casseroles. Buy the best quality you can afford so they are durable and will last a lifetime. Seek out a heavy iron pot that can be used on the stovetop and also in the oven. If you buy just one piece of equipment, this is the one-pot essential to invest in.

I love my 12-inch heavy, black Le Creuset pot with a tight-fitting lid. It's chic enough to bring to the table and large enough to make a stew or tagine to feed everyone for a family supper or to share with friends for dinner. If you're cooking for smaller numbers, an 8½-inch round or 10-inch oval enamel casserole is also a good investment.

A 1.25-quart Pyrex pie dish is perfect for sweet or savory puddings, such as Indian Rice Pudding (page 191) and savory bread puddings such as Gruyère, Piquillo Pepper & Basil Bread & Butter Pudding (page 139).

Several heavy enamel baking sheets with a lip, a good stainless steel roasting pan and a couple of gratin dishes, which could be Pyrex, pottery, earthenware, or stainless steel, are perfect for the Soda Bread Pizza (page 160) or Toad in the Hole (page 83). Le Creuset also make a gratin dish (8¼ x 11½ inches) that I use again and again for dishes like Roast Scallops (page 97) or Roasted Peaches, Nectarines, or Apricots with Honey & Lavender (page 184). I also love my lidded, heavy, stainless-steel Penthole sauté pans that can go on the stovetop and in the oven, as used in a number of recipes. I have two sizes: 8½ inches and 10½ inches. They even double up as cake pans.

EGGS

There are so many variations on this much-loved Middle Eastern dish, which is also a favorite around the Mediterranean and Tunisia. This makes a fantastic Sunday brunch or supper dish.

Shakshuka

- ½–1 teaspoon caraway seeds
- 3½ tablespoons extra virgin olive oil, plus extra to drizzle
- 1 medium onion, thinly sliced
- 1 red pepper, seeded and thinly sliced
- 1 teaspoon chili flakes
- 1 teaspoon ground cumin
- 1 teaspoon sweet smoked paprika, to taste
- 2 large ripe tomatoes, chopped
- 2 x 14-ounce cans of plum tomatoes, chopped
- 8 organic, free-range eggs
- 1¾ ounces feta cheese
- 2 tablespoons chopped cilantro leaves
- sea salt flakes, freshly ground black pepper, and a pinch of sugar
- sourdough bread, to serve

Preheat the oven to 400°F.

Sprinkle the caraway seeds into a 10-inch heavy, ovenproof frying pan and toast over medium heat for 2–3 minutes until the seeds become a shade darker and smell fragrant. Add the extra virgin olive oil and continue to cook for a further minute or two. Reduce the heat.

Add the sliced onion and red pepper and cook for 5–8 minutes until soft and jammy. Add the chili flakes, cumin, and paprika and cook for a further 3–4 minutes, stirring.

Stir in the chopped tomatoes and cook for 5 minutes before adding the canned tomatoes and a pinch of sugar. Bring slowly to a boil and season with salt and pepper. Reduce the heat to low and simmer gently for 20–25 minutes until the sauce is thick, rich, and delicious.

Take a wooden spoon and hollow out eight little "wells" in the surface of the sauce for the eggs. Crack in the eggs and, taking care not to break the yolks, use a spoon to bury the egg whites gently under the sauce—leaving the yolks uncovered. Crumble the feta over the egg whites (not the yolks) and drizzle with extra virgin olive oil.

Transfer the pan to the oven and bake for 5 minutes for "just set" yolks and 7–8 minutes for harder yolks.

Remove from the oven. Sprinkle with plenty of cilantro, drizzle with extra virgin olive oil, and season with a sprinkling of sea salt flakes.

Serve with lots of fresh or toasted sourdough for dipping.

SERVES 4

A super "master" recipe, also known as shirred eggs, or simply as baked eggs. Nothing could be simpler: take a few eggs and a few good things from your refrigerator or pantry, combine everything together, and tuck in. There are infinite variations—just make sure your eggs are super-fresh and the cream is rich and unctuous.

Baked eggs *with smoked mackerel & dill*

- 1 tablespoon butter
- 2 smoked mackerel fillets, broken into flakes
- 2 tablespoons chopped dill
- 6–8 tablespoons heavy cream
- 4 organic, free-range eggs
- sea salt flakes and freshly ground black pepper
- chopped flat-leaf parsley and pul biber (Aleppo pepper)
- crusty bread (optional), to serve

Lightly butter a 7½-inch round or oval gratin dish. Sprinkle the smoked mackerel and dill over the base. Pour half of the cream into the dish and carefully break in the eggs. Season with salt and pepper. Spoon the remaining cream over the top.

Place the dish in a bain-marie of hot water, cover with a lid and bring to a simmer on the stovetop. Continue to cook either gently on the stovetop or, uncovered, in a moderate oven at 350°F for about 10 minutes for a soft egg, or 12 minutes for a firmer egg.

Serve immediately, sprinkled with chopped parsley and pul biber. Accompany with some crusty bread, if you wish.

Variations

CHEESY BAKED EGGS

Follow the recipe above, omitting the mackerel and dill. Top each egg with ½–1 tablespoon of finely grated Parmesan, Gruyère or Cheddar cheese (or a mixture) and bake, uncovered, in a bain-marie in the oven as in the recipe above.

BAKED EGGS WITH YOGURT & PAPRIKA OIL

Follow the recipe for Cheesy Baked Eggs, omitting the cheese. After the creamy eggs come out of the oven, top each one with a dollop of plain yogurt and drizzle with paprika oil (made by gently heating 1 teaspoon of sweet or smoked paprika with 4 tablespoons of extra virgin olive oil).

BAKED EGGS WITH ANCHOVIES & PUL BIBER

Lightly butter a 7½-inch round or oval gratin dish and add 4 tablespoons of heavy cream. Crack in 4 eggs and lay a beautiful anchovy on top of each. Top each with another spoonful of cream and sprinkle with pul biber (Aleppo pepper) or, better still, a mixture of pul biber and some freshly roasted ground cumin. Bake in a bain-marie in the oven, as above, and serve scattered with freshly chopped flat-leaf parsley.

OEUFS EN COCOTTE WITH TOMATO FONDUE

Lightly butter a 7½-inch round or oval gratin dish and put 4 tablespoons of Tomato Fondue (page 133) in the bottom. Top with 4 eggs and spoon over 4 tablespoons of heavy cream. Season with salt and pepper and top each egg with ½–1 tablespoon of finely grated cheese. If you wish, include a little cooked bacon or some diced chorizo. Bake, uncovered, in a bain-marie in the oven as above.

This riff on the classic French omelet is one of my favorites. I've added some spices, but you can have fun dreaming up your own flavors and additions. The quintessential fast food, this Masala omelet is tender and delicious—and oozing with flavor.

Masala omelet

- 1 ripe tomato, finely chopped
- ¼ teaspoon green chili, finely chopped
- 1 tablespoon chopped cilantro (leaves and stalks), plus extra to garnish
- 2 organic, free-range eggs
- 2 teaspoons whole milk or water
- ¼ teaspoon ground cumin
- ¼ teaspoon ground coriander
- a pinch of ground turmeric
- 1 tablespoon chopped scallion
- 2 teaspoons extra virgin olive oil or clarified butter (see below)
- hot sauce (optional), to serve
- sea salt flakes, freshly ground black pepper, and a pinch of sugar

CLARIFIED BUTTER
Melt 1 cup of butter gently in a saucepan or in a Pyrex pitcher in a low oven at 300°F. Let stand for a few minutes, then spoon the crusty white layer of salt particles off the top of the melted butter. Underneath this crust there is clear liquid butter, which is called clarified butter. The milky liquid at the bottom can be discarded or used in a white sauce. Clarified butter is excellent for cooking because it can withstand a higher temperature when the salt and milk solids are removed. It will keep, covered, in the refrigerator for several weeks.

Warm a serving plate in the oven. Season the chopped tomato with salt, pepper, and sugar.

Preheat a 9-inch nonstick omelet pan over the highest heat. Have the tomato and chili ready beside you, along with a spoon and a plastic spatula and the chopped cilantro.

Whisk the eggs, milk or water and the spices, scallion, and chili in a bowl until thoroughly combined, but not too fluffy. Season with salt and pepper. Put the warmed plate beside the stovetop because you won't have time to go looking for it later.

Add the clarified butter or olive oil to the pan. As soon as it sizzles, pour in the egg mixture. It will start to cook immediately, so quickly pull the edges of the omelet toward the center with a plastic spatula, tilting the pan backward and forward, then up and down for another few seconds so that the uncooked egg runs to the sides. Continue right around the pan until most of the egg is set and it will not run easily any more. The center should still be soft and moist—don't worry, it will be perfectly set by the time it gets to the table. Sprinkle the seasoned tomato, chili, and chopped cilantro over the surface of the omelet.

To fold the omelet, use the spatula to flip the omelet edge nearest the handle of the pan over the filling, toward the center. Then change your grip of the handle so you are holding it from underneath; this will make it more comfortable for you to hold as you tilt it upright. Tilt the pan so it is almost upright and, hey presto, the top of omelet will roll toward the bottom of the pan.

Half-roll and half-slide the omelet onto the plate so that it lands folded into three. Garnish with a couple of sprigs of cilantro. Serve immediately with a salad of organic greens, some good bread, a glass of wine, and maybe a dash of hot sauce, if you wish.

A cross between a pancake and an omelet, these roll-ups are fast and fun to make with family and friends.

Variations

SMOKED MACKEREL, DILLISK & CHIVES

Omit the ground spices, chili, and scallion and replace with 2 tablespoons of smoked mackerel flakes, a generous sprinkle of dried dillisk (dulse seaweed), and freshly chopped chives. Sprinkle the flaked mackerel, dillisk, and chopped chives on the omelet just before folding. Save a little extra for garnish.

TOMATO FONDUE & BOCCONCINI—WITH OR WITHOUT PESTO

Omit the ground spices, chili, and scallion and replace with 2 tablespoons of hot Tomato Fondue (page 133) and 4–5 bocconcini. Add the tomato fondue and bocconcini, fold. Sprinkle over some basil and flat-leaf parsley leaves to garnish.

A LITTLE 'NDUJA & FLAT-LEAF PARSLEY

Omit the ground spices, chili, and scallion and replace with a filling of 2 tablespoons of diced 'nduja and 1 tablespoon of chopped flat-leaf parsley. Fold and garnish with extra chopped parsley.

TANSY

Adding tansy to the eggs is a revelation. Follow the main recipe, omitting the ground spices, scallion and chili and replacing them with 1 teaspoon of chopped tansy added to the egg mixture.

Omelet *roll-ups*

- 4 organic, free-range eggs
- 2 tablespoons water or whole milk
- 2 tablespoons extra virgin olive oil or clarified butter (page 16)
- sea salt flakes and freshly ground black pepper
- arugula leaves, to serve

FOR THE FILLING
- a small handful of organic salad greens per person
- ½ cucumber, peeled, and cut into long sticks
- 2–3 tablespoons sliced scallions
- 1–2 avocados, peeled, pitted, and sliced
- 3–4 tomatoes, sliced and seasoned with salt, pepper, and a sprinkling of sugar
- tomato relish, to serve (optional)

Whisk together the eggs and milk or water in a bowl. Season with salt and pepper.

Preheat a 10-inch nonstick pan over the highest heat and add a dash of extra virgin olive oil or clarified butter. Pour enough of the egg mixture into the pan to coat the base evenly—it should sizzle and set almost immediately. Flip the omelet over and cook the other side for a few seconds, then slide it out of the pan onto a plate.

Repeat the process until all of the omelet mixture is used up, stacking the omelets on top of one another.

Fill the omelets with the fillings of your choice, then roll them up and serve on a bed of arugula leaves.

This was a favorite Allen family supper dish when I first came to Ballymaloe in the late 1960s. It was simply called Flat Omelet...but after a Danish intern told us it was exactly like the omelet her family enjoyed on Funen, it was renamed Danish Omelet and so it has been ever since.

Danish family omelet

- 8 large organic, free-range eggs
- 2 tablespoons water
- 1¾ tablespoons butter
- 4 tablespoons diced cooked ham, bacon, chorizo, or merguez
- 1 generous tablespoon freshly chopped flat-leaf parsley
- 1 tablespoon freshly chopped chives
- sea salt flakes and freshly ground black pepper
- tomato salad and green salad, to serve

Crack the eggs into a large bowl, add the water, and season generously with salt and pepper. Whisk vigorously until the mixture fluffs up and increases in volume by three or four times.

Melt the butter in a 10-inch metal or nonstick frying pan over medium heat. When it foams, swirl the butter around the sides of the pan. Pour in the egg mixture, reduce the heat, and cook for 6–7 minutes until the bottom is set. Don't stir.

Sprinkle the cooked ham, bacon, chorizo, or merguez over the top. It will sink through the frothy surface. Scatter with the freshly chopped herbs, but don't fold them in.

Serve immediately from the pan while still warm. I bring the pan to the table and serve the omelet in segments alongside a tomato salad and some organic leaves.

Good things to add to a frittata

PEA SHOOTS, PEAS & MINT

Follow the main recipe, replacing the meat, goat cheese, and tomatoes with 2 handfuls of pea shoots, a cup of cooked peas, and 1–2 tablespoons of chopped mint.

WILD GARLIC

Follow the main recipe, replacing the meat, goat cheese, and tomatoes with 2 handfuls of chopped wild garlic leaves. Garnish with wild garlic flowers, if available.

CHILI & CILANTRO

Follow the main recipe, omitting the herbs and replacing the meat, goat cheese, and tomato with ½–1 diced red chili and 1 tablespoon of freshly chopped cilantro.

SMOKED SALMON & GOAT CHEESE

Follow the main recipe, replacing the meat and tomatoes with 3¾–6 ounces diced smoked salmon. Replace the herbs with fresh dill.

ROAST PUMPKIN, GOAT CHEESE & ARUGULA

Follow the main recipe, replacing the meat and tomatoes with 1¼ pounds diced roasted pumpkin and 2 handfuls of arugula.

ZUCCHINI BLOSSOM & MINT

Follow the main recipe, replacing the meat, goat cheese, and tomatoes with 6 ounces diced and sautéed zucchini, 1 cup of zucchini blossoms, torn into pieces, and 1–2 tablespoons of chopped mint. Tarragon is delicious here also but use sparingly.

ASPARAGUS, ARUGULA & WILD GARLIC

Follow the main recipe, replacing the meat, goat cheese, and tomatoes with 5½ ounces blanched asparagus tips, a handful of arugula and 4 tablespoons of chopped wild garlic leaves.

Every teenager should be able to whip up a frittata before they leave school. It's a brilliant basic recipe to have in your repertoire, a one-pan dish that will feed family and friends. It can, of course, be super simple with just a few fresh herbs and cheese—or you could go all out with some delicious chunky morsels of smoked fish or spicy sausage, goat cheese or bocconcini, cherry tomatoes and fresh basil leaves. Enjoy for breakfast, lunch, dinner, or a picnic, or cut into cubes to serve with drinks. A frittata can be served directly from the pan for a rustic family meal. Frittata were originally cooked on the stovetop, but nowadays I prefer to bake mine gently in the oven.

Chorizo, goat cheese & tomato frittata

- 10 large organic, free-range eggs
- 1 teaspoon sea salt flakes and lots of freshly ground black pepper
- 2 tablespoons chopped flat-leaf parsley
- 2 teaspoons thyme leaves
- 2 tablespoons freshly chopped basil or marjoram
- 2¾ ounces Gruyère cheese, grated
- 1 ounce Parmesan cheese, grated
- 3¾–6 ounces chorizo, merguez, or saucisses de Toulouse, cut into ½-inch dice
- 1 pound cherry tomatoes, halved
- 1¾ tablespoons butter
- 3¾ ounces goat cheese

TO SERVE
- arugula leaves
- extra virgin olive oil
- either a good green salad or a tomato and basil leaf salad

Crack the eggs into a bowl and whisk in the salt, freshly ground black pepper, fresh herbs, and grated cheeses. Carefully fold in the chorizo and tomatoes.

Melt the butter in a 9-inch nonstick frying pan and when it starts to foam, tip in the well-whisked eggs. Then arrange the goat cheese in dollops evenly over the top.

THERE ARE TWO COOKING METHODS:
Either Reduce the heat as low as it will go and leave the eggs to cook gently on a heat diffuser mat for 12 minutes, or until the underneath is set. The top should still be slightly runny. Then pop the pan under a preheated broiler for 1 minute just to set the surface, but don't let it brown.
Or After an initial 3–4 minutes on the stovetop, transfer the pan to a preheated oven at 325°F for 15–20 minutes, or until the frittata is just set. I prefer this method.

To turn out the frittata, slide a palette knife underneath to free it from the pan and carefully slide it onto a warm plate.

To serve, cut into wedges and arrange some arugula leaves with a drizzle of extra virgin olive oil on top. Accompany with a good green salad or perhaps a tomato and basil leaf salad.

A tasty little supper in a frying pan. I use a lovely hand-forged pan for this one, which I like to bring to the table—but if you'd rather not, you can simply slide the contents onto a warm serving plate and enjoy.

Fried eggs *with red pepper & chorizo*

- 2 tablespoons extra virgin olive oil
- 1 small onion, finely sliced
- 1 medium red bell pepper, seeded and cut into ¾-inch squares
- ½–1 red chili, seeded and thinly sliced
- 4 organic, free-range eggs
- a pinch of pul biber/Aleppo pepper (optional)
- 1 avocado, peeled, pitted, and cut into 1-inch chunks
- 2 tablespoons diced chorizo
- 2 tablespoons sliced scallions
- 2 tablespoons chopped cilantro
- sea salt flakes and freshly ground black pepper

Heat the oil in a 12-inch nonstick frying pan over medium heat and add the onion, red pepper, and chili. Season well with salt and pepper. Cover and cook for 4–5 minutes, stirring occasionally, until almost soft. Transfer to a plate, wipe out the pan and pop it back on the stovetop with a generous layer of extra virgin olive oil.

Crack the eggs into the pan, and season generously with salt, freshly ground black pepper, and a pinch of pul biber. Cover the pan with a lid and cook for 4–5 minutes until the whites are set, but the yolks are still nicely soft.

Sprinkle the onion, bell pepper, and chili mixture over the top and add some chunks of avocado and diced chorizo. Scatter over the scallions and cilantro and serve as soon as possible.

Other good sprinkles

SMOKED MACKEREL OR SALMON
Follow the recipe above, replacing the avocado and chorizo with 2 tablespoons of diced smoked salmon. Replace the cilantro with 2 tablespoons of chopped dill.

TOMATO & CHERVIL
Follow the recipe above, replacing the chorizo with 2–3 tablespoons of diced very ripe tomato and replace the cilantro with 2 tablespoons of chopped chervil.

POTATO & OLIVE
Follow the recipe above, replacing the chorizo with 4½ ounces (about 1 cup) diced cooked potatoes and the avocado with 6 pitted Kalamata olives.

SERVES 2

For many of us, scrambled eggs are the perennial standby—a tasty breakfast or supper dish, made in minutes, delicious unadorned but also a vehicle for all sorts of morsels from the refrigerator. Soft folds of scrambled egg are rare indeed. For perfection, really fresh free-range eggs are essential. Perfectly scrambled eggs need no further embellishment, except perhaps some hot toast and lots of freshly cracked pepper. I adore the luxurious combination of Lough Neagh smoked eel and softly scrambled eggs, but smoked mackerel or wild smoked salmon also work beautifully.

Scrambled eggs *with smoked fish & chervil*

- 4 organic, free-range eggs
- 2 tablespoons creamy milk or light cream
- a pat of butter
- 8 ounces Irish smoked salmon, mackerel, or eel, cut into ¾-inch dice
- 1 tablespoon chopped chervil, plus a few extra sprigs to garnish
- 1 tablespoon grated Parmesan cheese
- sea salt flakes and freshly ground black pepper

Break the eggs into a bowl, add the milk or cream, and season with salt and pepper. Whisk thoroughly until the whites and yolks are well mixed.

Put a dollop of butter into a cold 8-inch low-sided, heavy-based saucepan, pour in the egg mixture and stir continuously over low heat, preferably with a flat wooden spoon, until the eggs have scrambled into soft creamy curds. Carefully fold in the smoked fish and chopped chervil.

Serve immediately on warm plates with a sprinkling of grated Parmesan and a few sprigs of fresh chervil on top. Accompany with lots of hot buttered sourdough toast or fresh soda bread. (Note: If the plates are too hot, the scrambled egg can actually overcook between the stovetop and the table.)

Delicious morsels to add to scrambled eggs

FINES HERBES

Follow the main recipe, replacing the smoked fish and chervil with 1 tablespoon of mixed fresh herbs, such as chives, flat-leaf parsley, tarragon, basil, chervil, cilantro, dill, or tansy.

CHILI OR HARISSA

Follow the main recipe, replacing the smoked fish and chervil with ½–1 teaspoon of diced or sliced red chili, or harissa and a herb of your choice.

SPICES

Follow the main recipe, replacing the smoked fish and chervil with ½–1 teaspoon of ground cumin and ½–1 teaspoon of ground coriander. Add or omit the sprinkling of Parmesan as you wish.

CHEESE

Follow the main recipe, replacing the smoked fish and chervil with 2–4 tablespoons of grated cheese, such as Cheddar, Monterey Jack, Gruyère, Parmesan or pecorino.

'NDUJA, CHORIZO OR BACON

Cut 2 ounces bacon or chorizo into ¼-inch dice and fry gently until the oil begins to release. Follow the main recipe, replacing the smoked fish with the 'nduja, fried bacon, or chorizo (the 'nduja doesn't need to be cooked). Add or omit the Parmesan as you wish.

SCALLIONS OR CHIVES

Follow the main recipe, replacing the smoked fish and chervil with 2 tablespoons of chopped scallions or chives.

SORREL, SPINACH, OR KALE

Blanch 8 ounces sorrel, spinach, or kale in boiling water for 2–3 minutes, refresh under cold running water, drain thoroughly and finely chop. Follow the main recipe, replacing the smoked fish and chervil with the sorrel, spinach, or kale.

FORAGED GREENS

Follow the recipe above, replacing the smoked fish and chervil with 8 ounces chopped wild garlic, sorrel, dandelion, or watercress, or a mixture.

CHANTERELLES OR YELLOW LEG MUSHROOMS

Fry 3¾ ounces mushrooms in ½–1 tablespoon of butter and season well. Follow the main recipe, replacing the smoked fish and chervil with the mushrooms.

MASALA SCRAMBLED EGG

Heat the butter over medium heat. Add ½ cup finely diced onion and ½ teaspoon of grated fresh ginger and sauté until the onion is soft. Add ½–1 diced red chili, 2 very ripe tomatoes, peeled and chopped, 2 teaspoons of ground cumin, 1 tablespoon of chopped cilantro, and ⅛ teaspoon of ground turmeric, then stir for a few seconds. Reduce the heat right down, add the whisked eggs and scramble as before. Garnish with a few sprigs of fresh cilantro.

SERVES 6

Another one-pot gem that makes a perfect lunch or supper dish. I bake this soufflé until golden and puffy in a shallow sauté pan instead of the traditional soufflé dish. The cheese needs to be really tasty. Pretty pink or purple thyme flowers are so lovely sprinkled over the top just before serving.

Goat cheese & thyme leaf soufflé

- 1¼ cups heavy cream
- 1¼ cups whole milk
- 1 small onion, quartered
- sprig of thyme, a few flat-leaf parsley stalks, and a little scrap of bay leaf
- ⅓ cup butter
- 4¾ tablespoons all-purpose flour
- 5 organic, free-range eggs, separated
- 1 cup crumbled goat cheese (I use St. Tola or Ardsallagh farmhouse goat cheese)
- ⅔ cup grated Gruyère cheese
- ⅔ cup grated aged Coolea* or Parmigiano Reggiano
- a good pinch of sea salt, freshly ground black pepper, cayenne, and nutmeg
- 2 teaspoons fresh thyme leaves and thyme flowers, in season, to garnish

*Good to know

Coolea is an award-winning Irish Gouda-type farmhouse cheese.

Preheat the oven to 450°F.

Pour the cream and milk into a heavy-based pan, add the onion and herbs, and bring almost to a boil. Turn off the heat and set aside to infuse for 15 minutes or so.

Melt the butter in a sauté pan, add the flour, and cook for a minute or two. Strain the hot, creamy milk into the pan, whisking continuously as it comes to a boil and thickens. Remove from the heat and set aside to cool slightly.

Beat in the egg yolks, goat cheese, Gruyère, and most of the Coolea (or Parmesan) and season to taste with salt, freshly ground black pepper, cayenne, and nutmeg.

In a separate bowl, whisk the egg whites until stiff peaks form and gently fold in the cheese sauce to make a loose consistency. Scatter the thyme leaves over the surface and sprinkle with the remaining Coolea (or Parmesan).

Cook in the hot oven for 20–25 minutes until the sides and top of the soufflé are nicely puffed up and golden—the center should still be creamy. Garnish with thyme flowers, if available.

Serve immediately on warm plates with a good green salad.

This version of eggy bread comes from Kolkata, where street vendors set up their street food stalls on Park Street and Fairlie Place in the business district at noon each day, collectively they will feed the hundreds of workers who pour out of their offices in search of tasty nourishing foods—this simple snack is filling and super delicious.

Indian French toast

- 4 thickish slices of good white bread
- 3–4 organic, free-range eggs
- 1 small onion, finely chopped
- 1 green chili, seeded and chopped
- 4 tablespoons chopped cilantro
- rock or sea salt and freshly ground black pepper
- olive oil, for frying

First lightly toast the bread (in Kolkata it is grilled over charcoal). Whisk the eggs in a flattish dish; add a pinch of salt and the finely chopped onion, green chili, and cilantro.

Dip one slice of bread into the egg, then flip over to make sure it is saturated on both sides.

Warm a little oil in a large frying pan until sizzling. Slap in the soaked bread.

Repeat with the remaining three slices and use up all the egg. Cook until crisp and golden on both sides. Cut into quarters, sprinkle generously with salt, and serve.

POULTRY

Thai chicken & *noodle coconut broth*

- 6 ounces flat rice stick noodles
- 1 x 14-ounce can best-quality coconut milk
- generous 2 cups homemade chicken stock
- 1 heaped tablespoon grated fresh ginger
- 1 fresh red chili, finely sliced
- 1 tablespoon chopped cilantro
- 1–2 tablespoons fish sauce
- 2 organic, free-range chicken breasts, boned and skinned
- 1 handful of fresh Thai basil leaves

TO SERVE
- 4 tablespoons thinly sliced scallion
- cilantro leaves

Pour boiling water over the noodles in a bowl. Cover and let sit for about 10 minutes. Drain and rinse immediately under cold water. Cut the noodles into ¾-inch lengths. Leave in the colander until you are ready to serve the soup.

Put the coconut milk, chicken stock, ginger, chili, cilantro, and fish sauce into a medium saucepan over medium heat. Bring to a boil and simmer gently for 10 minutes, then reduce the heat so the broth is barely bubbling.

Meanwhile, cut the chicken breasts across into ⅛-inch slivers. Add the sliced chicken to the broth and cook very gently for 3–4 minutes until the chicken slices change color and are just cooked through. Adjust the seasoning, adding a little extra fish sauce if necessary. Throw in the basil leaves and let stand for a few minutes.

Pour a kettle of boiling water over the noodles in the colander and drain well.

Warm 4–6 wide deep bowls and divide the noodles between them. Top with the chicken and ladle over the hot coconut broth. Serve at once, scattered with scallions and fresh cilantro. A few lime wedges can be nice as well.

If asparagus is in season, slice 4–6 trimmed spears at an angle and add them to the pot 4–5 minutes before the end of the cooking time for extra deliciousness in this spring pot. Florets of Romanesco in season are another of my top additions to this dish.

A spring chicken *in a pot*

- 6 large organic, free-range chicken thighs or drumsticks
- 2 tablespoons extra virgin olive oil
- 2 medium onions, roughly chopped
- 2 cups homemade chicken stock
- 12 small new potatoes
- a sprig of thyme
- 1 Hispi or spring cabbage, finely sliced
- 1 cup shelled peas
- 1 tablespoon chopped tarragon
- 4 scallions, sliced
- 2 tablespoons coarsely chopped flat-leaf parsley
- sea salt flakes and freshly ground black pepper
- 4–5 tablespoons heavy cream or crème fraîche (optional)

Season the chicken pieces well with salt and pepper.

Heat the olive oil in a 4-quart heavy casserole over medium-high heat, add the chicken, and brown lightly on all sides.

Stir in the onions, then add the well-flavored stock, potatoes, and a nice sprig of thyme. Season with salt and pepper. Bring to a boil, then cover with a lid and simmer for 30 minutes.

Remove the thyme sprig, add the cabbage, and simmer gently for a further 5–6 minutes, uncovered. Add the peas and tarragon and cook for another couple of minutes. Stir in half of the scallions and parsley, saving the rest to scatter over the top. Season to taste, add the cream or crème fraîche (if using) and serve.

There are many versions of this Georgian pheasant recipe. We particularly love to make it with wild pheasant, which has lots of gamey flavor, and walnuts from the tree at the end of the garden that I planted myself over twenty-five years ago and am inordinately proud of.

Faisinjan

- 2 plump pheasants, each cut into 4 portions
- 2 tablespoons extra virgin olive oil
- 1 onion, chopped
- 1 x 2–3-inch cinnamon stick
- 2¼ cups shelled walnuts, finely chopped but gritty
- 3 tablespoons pomegranate syrup
- 2 cups homemade chicken or pheasant stock
- 2 tablespoons chopped flat-leaf parsley
- sea salt flakes, freshly ground black
  pepper, and sugar, to taste

Season the pheasant pieces with salt and pepper.

Heat the oil in a 10-inch frying pan over medium heat and brown the pheasant pieces on all sides. Transfer to a plate.

Add the onion to the pan and fry until pale golden brown, stirring regularly to prevent burning. Reduce the heat and add the cinnamon stick and walnuts. Cook gently for a few minutes, stirring, then add the pomegranate syrup and stock. Bring to a boil, stirring.

Add the pheasant pieces back to the pan, then cover the pan with a lid and simmer gently for 30 minutes. Uncover and continue to cook over gentle heat for 15–30 minutes until the meat is very tender and the sauce is thick. Taste and add more salt or pepper and a little sugar, if necessary, to balance the sauce. It should taste sweet and sour.

To serve, sprinkle with the chopped parsley and accompany with a good green salad and a big bowl of mashed potato or rice, if you wish.

- 1 x approx. 4½-pound organic chicken

- 4½-pound selection of chunky
  vegetables of your choice, such as:
  carrots, peeled and cut into 1½in chunks
  parsnips, peeled and cut into 1½in chunks
  pumpkin or butternut squash, peeled
    and cut into 1½in chunks (optional)
  Jerusalem artichokes, peeled and cut
    into 1½in chunks
  red onions, peeled and cut into quarters
    or sixths depending on size
  beet, peeled and cut into 1½in chunks
  celeriac, peeled and cut into 1½in chunks
  leeks, cut into 1in slices
- extra virgin olive oil
- 8 whole garlic cloves, unpeeled
- sea salt and freshly ground black pepper
- 2 tablespoons rosemary or thyme leaves,
  plus extra fresh herbs, such as
  chervil, flat-leaf parsley, chives,
  to garnish

FOR THE MARINADE
- 1 tablespoon rosemary, chopped
- 4 garlic cloves, crushed
- 1 teaspoon freshly ground black pepper
- ½ teaspoon chili flakes (pul biber/
  Aleppo pepper, or Espelette pepper)
- ½ tablespoon freshly squeezed
  organic lemon juice
- 4 tablespoons extra virgin olive oil
- 1 teaspoon sea salt flakes or more
  if needed

- Gremolata or Pangrattato (optional
  accompaniment—see pages 70 and 101)

When you master this simple technique, it creates so many possibilities—a plump chicken, duck, or even a turkey, will roast in half the time. I have so much fun doing riffs on this recipe—how about Moroccan or Tunisian, Nordic, Georgian, Persian, or Baltic flavors—to whet your appetite just a little. At its simplest, just drizzle the skin side of your bird with extra virgin olive oil and scatter with freshly chopped rosemary or thyme leaves. Maybe add a sprinkling of pul biber (Aleppo pepper) or slather the skin with harissa or smoked paprika oil, or a masala oil to introduce a taste of India. Roasting the chicken over the pan of chunky root vegetables allows the juices and chicken fat to enhance the taste of the vegetables even further. Depending on the flavor, you may want to sprinkle it with gremolata or pangrattato—optional, but a delicious addition.

Spatchcock chicken
with rosemary & chili oil

First spatchcock the chicken. To spatchcock or butterfly the bird, remove the wishbone from the neck end (save for stock). Lay the chicken, breast side down, on a cutting board. Use a poultry shears to remove the back bone by cutting along both sides (chop the bone into 4 or 5 pieces and use to make a stock for gravy later). Then flip the chicken, breast side up, and rotate the legs so the drumsticks point outward. Press down firmly on the breast bone several times to flatten the bird. Tuck the wing tips behind the breast to make a neat shape. Trim the excess neck fat from the bird and add to the stock.
If this all seems too much to tackle, ask your butcher to spatchcock the chicken for you.

Next make the marinade. Mix the rosemary, garlic, pepper, chili flakes, lemon juice, and extra virgin olive oil together in a bowl. Just before cooking, brush the chicken both inside and out with the marinade. Put the chicken, skin side up on a wire rack. Sprinkle with sea salt flakes and allow to absorb the flavors for as long as you can spare, at least 30 minutes.

Meanwhile, preheat the oven 350°F.

Slide the rack into the oven and cook the chicken, skin side up, for about 45 minutes.

Meanwhile, prepare the selection of vegetables. Transfer to a roasting pan with the garlic cloves and drizzle with extra virgin olive oil. Season generously with salt and pepper. Sprinkle with chopped rosemary or thyme leaves. Toss well until the vegetables are evenly coated. Slide the roasting pan of vegetables (or just potatoes if you prefer) underneath the rack with the chicken and cook for 20–35 minutes or until the vegetables are soft and slightly caramelized. Make sure the chicken is fully cooked through.

To serve, carve the chicken into portions and serve on top of the roast vegetables or potatoes scattered with some freshly chopped herbs—chervil, parsley, chives—or the gremolata or pangrattato, if you wish. Serve with a good green salad.

SERVES 6

I sometimes use scraps from the chicken carcass from the stockpot for this recipe, but you could use raw or cooked chicken (either brown or white meat). Provide a platter of good things alongside—avocado, tomato, red onion, green chili, fresh cilantro, tortilla chips, and segments of fresh lime—for your family and friends to add to their broth as they choose.

Mexican chicken broth
with many good things

- 7¾ cups well-flavored and well-skimmed homemade chicken stock
- 8 ounces uncooked or cooked, shredded chicken (I prefer to use brown meat)
- sea salt flakes and freshly ground black pepper

TO SERVE

- 6 medium red tomatoes, cut into ½-inch dice
- 2–3 ripe Hass avocados, cut into ¾-inch dice
- 2 medium red onions, cut into ½-inch dice
- 2 green Serrano or Jalapeño chilies, thinly sliced
- 3 organic limes, cut into wedges
- 3–4 soft corn tortillas or a large bag of good-quality tortilla chips
- 4–6 tablespoons coarsely chopped cilantro leaves

Put the chicken stock into a wide 2½-quart saucepan and bring to a boil. Taste and season with salt and pepper—the stock should have a full rich flavor, otherwise the soup will be bland and insipid.

Just before serving, add the shredded chicken to the hot broth and poach gently so it doesn't toughen. Cooked chicken just needs to be heated through in the broth. Raw white meat will take 2–3 minutes to cook and brown meat a little longer—4–6 minutes. Season to taste.

I like to bring the soup to the table in a soup tureen. To serve, ladle into soup bowls and serve with your chosen accompaniments.

This roast cauliflower is delicious on its own but also pretty irresistible with some spicy chicken drumsticks. Look out for pul biber, not too hot but really aromatic. I fell in love with them on my first trip to Turkey.

Roast cauliflower *with saffron &* *bay leaves* & crispy chicken

- 4–8 organic, free-range chicken thighs or drumsticks, depending on size
- extra virgin olive oil
- ½–1 teaspoon rosemary, chopped
- 2 pinches of saffron strands
- 1 large or 2 small cauliflowers (approx. 2¼ pounds), leaves snapped off*, head broken into small florets, stalk roughly chopped
- 2 medium onions, finely sliced
- 1 tablespoon pul biber (Aleppo pepper) or a good pinch of dried chili flakes
- 3 bay leaves
- ⅓ cup golden raisins, soaked in hot water to plump up
- ⅓ cup almonds, coarsely chopped
- sea salt flakes and freshly ground black pepper

TO SERVE
- 2 tablespoons roughly chopped flat-leaf parsley
- 4 scallions, sliced on the diagonal

Preheat the oven to 400°F.

Slash the chicken drumsticks. Drizzle with a little extra virgin olive oil. Season with salt and pepper. Sprinkle with chopped rosemary, toss, and arrange in a single layer in a roasting pan. Roast for 30–45 minutes, depending on size, while you prepare the cauliflower.

Put the saffron into a little bowl, cover it with a couple of teaspoons of boiling water and leave it to steep. Put the cauliflower, onions, chili flakes, and bay leaves into a bowl and season with salt and pepper.

Once the saffron has steeped, add to the cauliflower mixture with the drained golden raisins and almonds. Transfer to the roasting pan and cover loosely with parchment paper to protect from burning. Bake for 20 minutes.

Remove the parchment and roast for a further 10–15 minutes until the edges are nicely caramelized, the cauliflower is tender, and the chicken is cooked. Turn into a shallow serving dish.

Sprinkle with the chopped parsley and scallions. Serve.

*Good to know
The leaves are also delicious roasted, add them a little later.

SERVES 6-8

A quickie that can be put together in a few minutes using your favorite curry powder. For the purpose of this one-pot book, we experimented by adding the rice to the curry close to the end of cooking. It works brilliantly and is super delicious.

Coconut curry chicken & *rice*

- 2 pounds organic, free-range chicken breast or thigh meat, cut into ½-inch chunks
- 3 tablespoons of your favorite curry powder
- 3 tablespoons extra virgin olive oil
- 5½ ounces onions, thinly sliced
- 2 garlic cloves, crushed
- generous 2½ cups coconut milk
- 1 x 14-ounce can of plum tomatoes, diced, and their juice
- 1 teaspoon sugar
- 1¾ cups basmati rice, soaked for 15-30 minutes in cold water and drained
- sea salt flakes and freshly ground black pepper

TO SERVE
- 1 lime, cut into wedges
- chopped cilantro
- 4-6 scallions, sliced on the diagonal

Season the chicken with salt and pepper. Mix together the curry power and oil in a small bowl. Heat a large saucepan, approx. 10 inches in diameter and 4 inches deep, over medium heat, add the curry oil mixture and stir for a minute or two. Add the onions and garlic and cook gently for 3 minutes until they start to color.

Add the chicken chunks and toss lightly to coat them with the curry oil mixture. Reduce the heat, cover with a lid, and simmer for 3-4 minutes, stirring occasionally.

Pour in the coconut milk, add the diced tomatoes and their juice and season with salt, freshly ground black pepper, and sugar. Bring to a boil, stirring, and then cover the pan with a lid and simmer gently until the chicken is cooked. Chicken breast should take 5-6 minutes; thigh meat will take a little longer, about 10-15 minutes. Sprinkle in the rice 6-8 minutes before the end of cooking. Remove the pan from the heat and set aside for 7 minutes, tightly covered with the lid, to allow the rice to swell.

To serve, squeeze over some lime juice to taste and sprinkle with fresh cilantro and lots of scallions. Accompany with a bowl of organic salad greens.

SERVES 6–8

This versatile one-pot winner also works with either drumsticks or thighs. Allow an extra 5–10 minutes for drumsticks in the oven—35–45 minutes in total. For best results with chicken thighs, slash each thigh three times right down to the bone to speed up the cooking time and encourage them to soak up all of the flavors.

Chicken wings *with tomato, pepper & harissa potatoes*

- 24 organic, free-range chicken wings, weighing approx. 3 pounds 2 ounces
- 1 heaped teaspoon chopped rosemary leaves
- 1 teaspoon thyme leaves
- 3½ tablespoons extra virgin olive oil
- 1 tablespoon harissa paste or smoked paprika
- 1 pound 2 ounces onions, cut into ½-inch slices
- 2¼ pounds potatoes, peeled and cut into ⅓-inch slices
- 1 pound red bell peppers, seeded and cut into ¾-inch squares
- 1 head of garlic, divided into cloves
- 2 sprigs of rosemary
- 2 generous sprigs of thyme
- 1 pound ripe tomatoes, cored and halved
- 1–2 teaspoons honey
- sea salt flakes and freshly ground black pepper

TO SERVE
- flat-leaf parsley or cilantro sprigs
- a sprinkling of smoked paprika

Preheat the oven to 450°F.

Tip the chicken wings into a large bowl and add the rosemary, thyme, ½ tablespoon of the extra virgin olive oil, and lots of sea salt. Rub the herby oil into the chicken wings and set aside.

Mix the harissa paste or smoked paprika with the remaining 3 tablespoons of extra virgin olive oil in a little bowl. Set aside.

Tip the sliced onions and potatoes into a roasting pan measuring approx. 15 x 13 x 1¼ inches. Add the red pepper and whole garlic cloves and drizzle with the harissa/paprika paste. Season, throw in the sprigs of rosemary and thyme and toss well to coat the vegetables. Spread out the vegetables in a single layer. Arrange the tomatoes on top of the vegetables. Season each tomato with salt and pepper, a drizzle of honey, and the remaining harissa/paprika paste.

Arrange the chicken wings in a single layer on an oven rack and slide into the oven. Slide the pan of vegetables into the oven, under the chicken wings so that the juices from the wings drip onto the vegetables. Roast the chicken wings for 30–35 minutes, turning them halfway through to crisp up on both sides. Once the wings are cooked through and crisp, remove them from the oven and set aside to rest.

Increase the temperature to 500°F and roast the vegetables for a further 10 minutes until nicely caramelized. Remove the vegetables from the oven and lay the crispy wings on top. Sprinkle with the cilantro sprigs and flat-leaf parsley and dust with a little more smoked paprika, if you fancy. Serve straight from the roasting pan.

POULTRY 43

Tumble all of the ingredients together in a bowl, season them well and toss them into a roasting pan for an irresistible one-dish supper.

Chicken supper in a dish *with aioli*

- 4½ pounds potatoes, such as Golden Wonder or Kerr's Pink
- 8–10 ounces medium onions, sliced into rings
- 8–10 large organic, free-range chicken legs, separated into thighs and drumsticks
- 1 large head of garlic, separated into cloves
- 1–2 tablespoons sweet or smoked paprika (or a mixture of both)
- 2 tablespoons chopped marjoram
- 3 tablespoons extra virgin olive oil
- juice of 1 organic lemon
- sea salt flakes and freshly ground black pepper

TO SERVE
- 3–4 large ripe tomatoes
- a dash of balsamic vinegar, to taste
- a dash of honey or sugar, to taste
- 3–4 sprigs of flat-leaf parsley
- Aioli (page 96)

Preheat the oven to 450°F.

Peel the potatoes and cut them into chunky wedges. Put them into a large bowl with the sliced onion rings, chicken pieces, and garlic cloves, and then sprinkle over the paprika, marjoram, and plenty of salt and pepper. Drizzle generously with the extra virgin olive oil and squeeze over the lemon juice. Toss thoroughly to coat the potatoes and the chicken in the flavorings. Spread in a single layer over a large roasting pan or a large gratin dish, approx. 14 x 16 inches.

Roast for 15–20 minutes, then reduce the heat to a moderate 350°F for a further 45 minutes or until the potatoes are golden and crisp at the edges and the chicken skin is sticky and irresistible. Check the chicken is cooked close to the bone; it may take a little longer.

Coarsely chop the tomatoes and place them in a small bowl. Season to taste with salt, freshly ground black pepper, balsamic vinegar, and honey (or sugar). Stir in the parsley. Sprinkle the tomato mixture over the hot chicken just as it comes out of the oven.

Accompany with the aioli and a salad of organic leaves anointed with a dressing of extra virgin olive oil and lemon juice.

This is a favorite way to cook pork in Italy, but the technique also works brilliantly with chicken, rose veal, or lamb. There is honestly no point in attempting this recipe if you cannot find a really good free-range bird. Cooking in milk produces the most delicious curdy liquid and the lactic acid in the milk has a tenderizing and moistening effect on the meat. Here, I've cooked the potatoes or rice in the milky juices—you can just imagine how delicious it all tastes.

Chicken *poached in milk*

- 4-pound organic, free-range chicken
- 1 tablespoon extra virgin olive oil
- thinly sliced peel from 1 organic lemon
- 1 teaspoon lightly crushed coriander seeds (or a small handful of fresh sage leaves)
- 4 garlic cloves, halved
- scant 4 cups whole milk
- a small bunch of marjoram
- 6–8 potatoes, peeled and halved or quartered, depending on size
  or 1–1¼ cups basmati rice, soaked for 15–30 minutes in cold water and drained
- sea salt flakes and freshly ground black pepper
- a few sprigs of chervil, to serve

Joint the chicken into 10 pieces and season generously with salt and pepper.

Heat the olive oil in a 3-quart/10-inch casserole over medium heat and brown the chicken pieces well on all sides. Remove them to a plate, then pour off the hot fat in the pan and discard.

Return the pan to a medium heat and add the lemon peel, coriander seeds (or sage), and garlic. Return the chicken pieces to the pan and pour in the milk so that it comes about halfway up the meat. Add the marjoram and bring to a boil.

Partially cover the pan with a lid and simmer gently over low heat for about 50 minutes, by which time the milk should have formed a golden skin. The liquid should simmer very gently all the time. The whole object of this exercise is to allow the milk to reduce slowly and form delicious, pale coffee-colored "curds" while the meat cooks.

If using potatoes, add them about 30 minutes into the start of the cooking time, scraping down any milk that has stuck to the sides of the pan at the same time. (If using rice, add after 45 minutes, scraping down any milk that has stuck to the sides of the pan. Cook for a further 6–7 minutes over low heat, then remove the pan from the heat, cover, and set aside for 5–10 minutes to allow the rice to swell.)

Serve the chicken with the precious curds spooned carefully over the top alongside the potatoes (or rice) and a scattering of chervil.

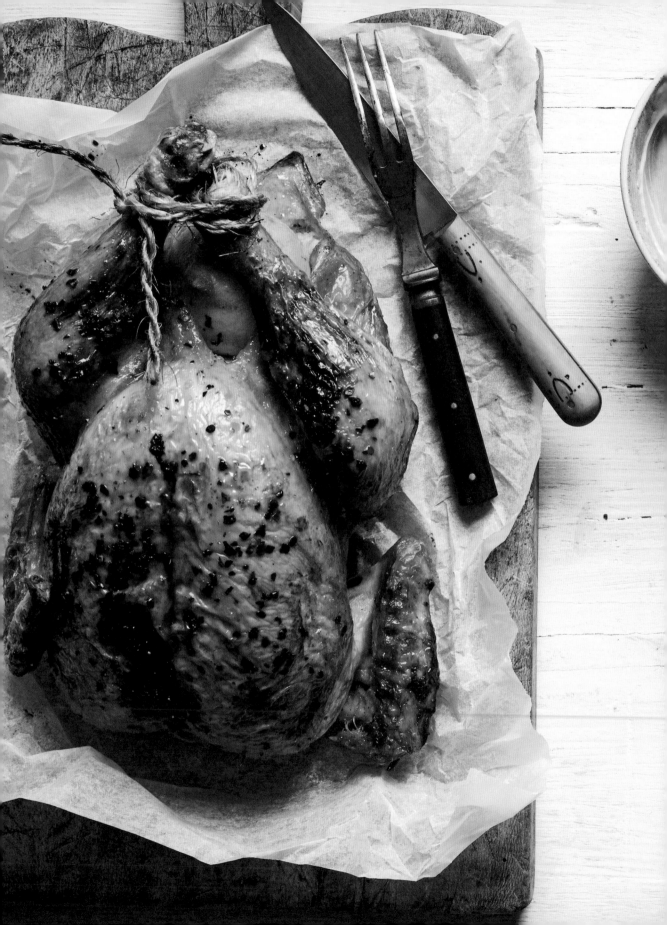

Crisp leaves of Little Gem lettuce provide the perfect scoops for chunks of tender chicken, drizzled with creamy Caesar dressing. This one is best served while the chicken is still a little warm.

Roast chicken salad *with* avocado & Caesar dressing

- 1 x 4–4½-pound organic, free-range chicken
- 2 organic lemons
- 2 tablespoons extra virgin olive oil
- 1 tablespoon clear honey
- 6 Little Gem lettuces
- 4 avocados
- 2 handfuls of watercress or wood sorrel
- sea salt flakes, freshly ground black pepper, and pul biber (Aleppo pepper)
- a handful of marigold petals, to garnish

Preheat the oven to 350°F.

Season the inside of the chicken with salt and pepper. Prick the lemons all over with a skewer and put them inside the chicken cavity. Tie the legs together and place the chicken in a medium roasting pan, approx. 13 x 12 inches. Drizzle the skin with the extra virgin olive oil.

Roast the chicken for 1½ hours, then brush the skin with honey, season with salt, freshly ground black pepper and a sprinkling of pul biber, and return to the oven for a further 15 minutes until the chicken is well-cooked and golden brown. Remove from the roasting pan and set aside to cool.

FOR THE CAESAR DRESSING

- 1 x 2-ounce can of anchovies
- 2 organic, free-range egg yolks
- 1 garlic clove, crushed
- 2 tablespoons freshly squeezed organic lemon juice
- a generous pinch of English mustard powder
- ½ teaspoon sea salt
- ½–1 tablespoon Worcestershire sauce
- ½–1 tablespoon Tabasco sauce
- scant ¾ cup sunflower oil
- 3½ tablespoons extra virgin olive oil
- 3½ tablespoons cold water

Meanwhile, make the dressing. I usually whiz up the Caesar dressing in a food processor, but you could also make it very quickly by hand. Drain the anchovies and crush them lightly with a fork. Place them in a food processor or medium-size bowl with the egg yolks, garlic, lemon juice, mustard powder, salt, and Worcestershire and Tabasco sauces. Whisk all of the ingredients together and then gradually start to whisk in the oils, adding them very slowly at first and then a little faster as the emulsion starts to form. Finally whisk in the water to make a spreadable consistency. Season to taste: this dressing should be highly flavored.

To serve, separate the leaves from the lettuces and arrange them over two platters. Remove each breast carefully from the chicken in one piece. Pull the meat from the legs and wings and tear it into chunky pieces. (Save the carcass to make stock.) Season the meat with salt and pepper. Cut each breast into 6 pieces, keeping the skin attached. Put a small spoonful of the brown meat into each lettuce leaf and top with a slice of breast meat. Halve, pit, and peel the avocado, then cut into quarters or sixths. Tuck a piece of avocado in among the chicken.

Just before serving, drizzle a little dressing over each piece of chicken. Garnish with a sprig of watercress or wood sorrel and sprinkle with the marigold petals, if available. Serve soon.

Any remaining dressing can be served as an accompaniment or stored in a lidded jar in the refrigerator for 10 days.

SERVES 8-10

Another dish that family and friends love me to cook
for them. A whole roasting pan of crispy chicken and
potatoes, perfumed with rosemary and thyme leaves.
My lips are smacking just thinking about it.

Roman chicken & fries
with rosemary & thyme

- 4½ pounds organic, free-range chicken
  thighs, drumsticks, and wings
- 2–3 tablespoons thyme leaves
- 1–2 tablespoons chopped rosemary
- 2½ pounds (about 10 large) potatoes
- extra virgin olive oil, to drizzle
- 9 ounces onions, sliced
- sea salt flakes and freshly ground
  black pepper

Preheat the oven to 450°F.

Season the chicken heavily with salt and pepper. Put into a
large bowl and scatter with the thyme leaves and chopped
rosemary, reserving some for the potatoes. Toss well.

Peel the potatoes and cut into ½-inch-thick fries. Dry and
season well with salt, freshly ground black pepper, and the
reserved thyme and chopped rosemary. Add to the bowl
with the chicken. Drizzle with extra virgin olive oil and toss
once again.

Scatter the sliced onions over the base of a roasting pan,
approx. 14½ x 12½ x ¾ inches, or two smaller pans approx.
12 x 8 x 1. Arrange the chicken and potatoes haphazardly on
top, making sure that the potatoes are popping up. Drizzle
with a little more olive oil.

Roast for 45 minutes–1 hour or until the chicken is cooked
through and the fries are crispy at the edges. (Organic chicken
pieces are often larger, so cooking time can be up to 1¼ hours.)

Serve from the pan, family style, with a good green salad and
several vegetables of your choice, if you wish.

*Good to know
One can add a little hot homemade chicken stock at the end
if the dish needs a little more juice.

Molley is an Indian dish that uses coconut and spices and is often made with fish, but here these flavors transform ground turkey into a totally irresistible one-pot meal. Gary Masterson, one of our tutors at the Ballymaloe Cookery School, shared this recipe and the one opposite with me.

Turkey molley

FOR THE MEATBALLS

- 2 tablespoons extra virgin olive oil
- 3¾ ounces (1 cup) finely chopped onions
- 9 ounces (generous 1 cup) ground turkey
- 2¾ ounces (about 1 cup) grated coconut
- ⅓ ounce (1 tbsp.) grated fresh ginger
- 1 teaspoon white wine vinegar
- ½ teaspoon sea salt

FOR THE SAUCE

- 3 tablespoons extra virgin olive oil
- 7 ounces (1¾ cups) finely chopped onions
- 6 garlic cloves, crushed
- 2 red chilies, finely diced
- 1 level teaspoon ground turmeric
- 5 medium tomatoes, quartered
- 7 ounces cauliflower, broken into
  ½–¾-inch florets
- 6 garlic cloves, sliced
- ⅓ ounce (1 tbsp.) grated fresh ginger
- ½ teaspoon sea salt
- 2 teaspoons white wine vinegar
- scant 1 cup coconut milk
- 3 green chilies, slit

FOR THE BANANA & YOGURT RAITA

- 2–3 tablespoons raisins or golden raisins
- 3 tablespoons blanched slivered almonds
- 3–4 green cardamom pods
- scant ½ cup plain yogurt
- 2½ tablespoons heavy cream
- 2½ tablespoons sour cream
- 2 teaspoons honey
- 2–4 firm ripe bananas, depending on size
- a pinch of salt

First prepare the meatballs. Heat the oil over medium heat in a 12-inch frying pan and gently fry the onion for 4–5 minutes until soft. Set aside to cool.

Combine the ground turkey, coconut, ginger, fried onion, vinegar, and salt in a large bowl. Shape into 16 meatballs the size of a small lime. Transfer to a plate, cover with plastic wrap, and set aside to firm up in the refrigerator for about an hour.

Meanwhile, make the raita. Pour boiling water over the raisins or golden raisins and set aside for 10 minutes. Toast the almonds (watch them: they burn really easily). Remove the seeds from the cardamom pods and crush in a pestle and mortar. Mix the yogurt with the creams and cardamom, add the honey, taste, and add more if needed. Add the drained raisins. Slice the bananas, season with a pinch of salt, and add to the yogurt base. Turn into a serving bowl and scatter with the toasted almonds, then chill for an hour if possible.

To make the sauce, heat the oil in the frying pan over lowish heat and fry the onion, crushed garlic, chili, turmeric, and tomatoes for 4–5 minutes until softened. Add the cauliflower, sliced garlic, ginger, salt, and vinegar, and cook for a further 3–4 minutes, stirring. Pour in the coconut milk, stir gently, and bring to a boil.

Tuck the meatballs into the sauce, then cover with a lid and simmer gently for about 15 minutes or until the meatballs are cooked through. Remove the lid, add the green chilies, and cook for a further 5 minutes until the sauce thickens. Season to taste.

Accompany with banana and cardamom raita, and some tomato chutney and flatbreads, if you wish.

These spices will transform the ground turkey into something irresistible, to scoop up with fresh lettuce leaves. Ground chicken can also be used; I prefer the brown meat but, of course, white meat is delicious too— just bear in mind that it needs a shorter cooking time.

Gary's Asian turkey lettuce wraps

- 2 tablespoons vegetable oil
- 1 ounce (3 tbsp.) grated fresh ginger
- 2 garlic cloves, crushed
- 2 red chilies, seeded and finely chopped
- 1 pound 2 ounces (2¼ cups) ground turkey (I use brown meat, but use white if you prefer)
- 4 kaffir lime leaves, shredded
- 3½ tablespoons palm sugar or light brown sugar
- juice of 1 organic lime
- 2 tablespoons fish sauce

ACCOMPANIMENTS
- 3–4 handfuls of Iceberg lettuce or 6 Little Gems halved
- a good handful of mint leaves
- a handful of cilantro leaves
- 2–3 shallots, finely sliced on the diagonal
- a handful of toasted peanuts or cashews, roughly chopped
- 1 organic lime, cut into wedges

Heat the oil over high heat in a large (10½-inch) frying pan. Add the ginger, garlic, and chilies and stir-fry for a minute or two to release their flavors. Add the ground turkey and cook over high heat until it starts to color, breaking it up with a wooden spoon as you go.

Add the kaffir lime leaves, sprinkle in the sugar, squeeze in the lime juice, and add 1 tablespoon of the fish sauce. Reduce the heat and cook everything down for 5–10 minutes until the mixture is sticky and delicious. Season to taste with the remaining fish sauce, if necessary.

To serve, transfer the filling to a serving bowl and accompany with little bowls of lettuce, herbs, shallots, peanuts or cashews, and lime wedges so that everyone can assemble their own little bundles.

This wonderful Moroccan dish, which Claudia Roden
made for us when she was guest chef at the school,
derives its name from the tomatoes in which it cooks
(there are mountains of them that reduce to a thick
sauce), and from the honey, which comes in at the end.

Moroccan chicken tagine
with tomatoes & honey

- 6 organic, free-range chicken legs
- 3 tablespoons extra virgin olive oil
- 8 ounces onions, diced (about 2 cups)
- 1 garlic clove, crushed
- 1 teaspoon ground cinnamon
- 1 teaspoon grated fresh ginger
- a pinch of saffron threads
- 3 pounds very ripe tomatoes, peeled
  and chopped, or canned chopped
  tomatoes
- 2 tablespoons honey
- sea salt flakes and freshly ground
  black pepper

FOR THE GARNISH
- ⅓ cup blanched almonds, toasted
- 1 tablespoon sesame seeds
- a few sprigs of cilantro

Separate the drumsticks from the thighs and season with salt
and pepper.

Heat the oil over medium heat in a wide 10-inch/3-quart
casserole and add the onion, garlic, and spices. Cook for
a minute or two, stirring, and then add the tomatoes and
chicken pieces. Cover and cook gently, stirring occasionally,
for about 1¼ hours until the chicken is meltingly tender.

Remove the chicken from the pan and set aside. Return the
tomato sauce to the stovetop and simmer gently, uncovered,
for about 20 minutes until the sauce thickens—it should be
concentrated and unctuous. The color will darken somewhat.
Stir regularly to prevent the sauce from sticking to the bottom
of the pan as the sugar in the tomatoes begins to caramelize.
Add the honey, then return the chicken to the casserole to
heat through.

Remove the chicken with a slotted spoon to a hot serving
dish, spoon over the sauce and garnish with the toasted
almonds, sesame seeds, and sprigs of fresh cilantro.

Everyone loves this spicy dish originally from Sichuan, known as Gong bao or Kung Po, but often better recognized by its American name "kung pao chicken". It can be super hot or a little less punchy, depending on the chilies, but don't dumb it down too much as the rice will absorb some of the heat.

Kung pao chicken

- 1 tablespoon cornstarch
- 4 tablespoons light soy sauce
- 1 pound organic, free-range chicken breast or thigh meat, cut into 1-inch cubes
- 3 tablespoons Shaoxing rice wine
- 2 tablespoons sugar
- 3 tablespoons homemade chicken stock
- 4 teaspoons Chinkiang rice vinegar
- 1 tablespoon sesame oil
- 2 teaspoons dark soy sauce
- 3 tablespoons peanut or sunflower oil

- 4–12 dried hot red chilies, halved crosswise and seeded
- 5 scallions (both white and green parts), sliced on the diagonal
- 1 large garlic clove, thinly sliced
- ½-inch piece of fresh ginger, grated
- ½ cup shelled peanuts
- fresh cilantro leaves
- 14 ounces (about 3½ cups) boiled basmati rice, to serve

- 12 ounces streaky bacon
- 1 x 3½-pound organic, free-range chicken (or 6 chicken thighs)
- a little extra virgin olive oil, for frying
- 1 pound baby onions, peeled and left whole
- 12 ounces carrots, peeled and thickly sliced (or left whole if they are small)
- 3¼ cups homemade chicken stock
- a sprig of fresh thyme
- sea salt flakes and freshly ground black pepper
- 2 tablespoons chopped flat-leaf parsley, to serve

FOR THE HERB CRUST
- 1¾ cups all-purpose flour
- ½ teaspoon sugar
- ½ teaspoon baking soda
- ½ teaspoon sea salt
- 1–2 tablespoons chopped mixed herbs, such as rosemary or sage and thyme, chives, flat-leaf parsley, or lemon balm
- ¾–scant 1 cup sour milk or buttermilk, to mix
- a little egg wash, made by beating 1 small organic, free-range egg with a pinch of salt, to glaze
- approx. ½ cup grated Cheddar cheese (optional)

Mix the cornstarch with 1 tablespoon of the light soy sauce in a medium bowl. Add the chicken cubes, toss well to coat and set aside to marinate for about 30 minutes.

Meanwhile, in a small bowl mix together the remaining light soy sauce, rice wine, sugar, chicken stock, vinegar, sesame oil, and dark soy sauce.

Heat the oil in a 12–14-inch wok or large frying pan over high heat until just beginning to smoke. Add the chilies, half the scallions, the garlic, ginger, and marinated chicken and stir-fry for 3–5 minutes until the chicken is golden. Add the soy sauce mixture and stir-fry for a further 2–3 minutes until the sauce begins to thicken. Stir in the peanuts. Scatter with the remaining scallions and lots of cilantro, and serve with the basmati rice, if you wish.

A good chicken casserole may sound a bit passé, but it always gets a hearty welcome from my family and friends. Sometimes I make an entire meal in a pot by covering the top with whole peeled potatoes just before it goes into the oven. If you don't have enough time to sauté the bacon and vegetables, just pop everything into the casserole, cover with chicken stock, and season well before you put it into the oven. This is a brilliant family meal with something for everyone in the pot: a baby starting on solid foods could have a little mashed potato and carrot with some of the rich juice; a little toddler will enjoy sucking on the bones and eating some of the larger pieces of vegetable and potato; and parents can enjoy the entire meal. No need for separate meals for children and adults with this one.

Super-easy chicken casserole *with a herb crust*

Preheat the oven to 350°F.

Remove the rind from the bacon (if necessary) and cut into ¾-inch cubes. Joint the chicken into 8 pieces and season well with salt and pepper.

Heat a little oil in a large, ovenproof casserole over medium heat and cook the bacon until crisp. Remove from the casserole and set aside. Add the chicken pieces to the casserole, a few at a time, and sauté until golden. Heat control is crucial here: the pan mustn't burn, yet it must be hot enough to sauté the chicken. If it is too cool, the chicken pieces will stew rather than sauté and as a result the meat may be tough. Once the chicken pieces are browned, remove from the casserole.

Toss the onions and carrots into the casserole, add a pat of butter, and cook for 1–2 minutes until coated. Return the meat to the casserole and pour in the stock. Season well with salt and pepper and pop in a sprig of thyme. Bring up to a boil, then cover with a lid. Transfer the casserole to the oven to cook for an initial 30 minutes while you make the herb crust.

To make the crust, sift the dry ingredients into a large bowl and add the freshly chopped herbs. Make a well in the center and pour in most of the milk, reserving some for later. Using one hand, gradually bring in the flour from the sides of the bowl and mix to a softish but not too wet and sticky dough, adding more milk if necessary. Turn out onto a floured surface, tidy the edges, and flip over. Roll the dough to a thickness of ¾ inch and stamp into rounds with a 2-inch cutter.

Once the casserole has cooked for 30 minutes, remove the lid and cover the surface of the stew with slightly overlapping herb scones. Brush with egg wash and sprinkle with a little cheese, if you wish. Increase the heat to 450°F and return to the oven for a further 10 minutes. Then reduce the heat to 400°F for a final 20 minutes or until the crust is baked and the chicken is cooked through.

Serve bubbling hot, sprinkled with some freshly chopped parsley.

Crisp duck legs, melting onions, and potatoes infused with thyme and duck juices—this is definitely one of my favorite winter suppers and it's brilliant for entertaining. Serve with a salad of winter leaves.

Duck legs *with potatoes, onions & thyme leaves*

- 4 organic, free-range duck legs
- extra virgin olive oil, for frying
- 2¼ pounds potatoes, peeled and cut into 1½-inch chunks
- 2¼ pounds medium onions, quartered or 1 pound white turnips, peeled and cut into chunks
- 2 teaspoons thyme leaves
- sea salt flakes and freshly ground black pepper
- sprigs of fresh thyme, to serve

Preheat the oven to 500°F.

Season the duck legs all over with the salt. Heat a tiny drop of oil in a heavy 10-inch/3-quart casserole and cook the duck, skin-side down, over medium heat until well browned. Turn and brown on the other side.

Remove the duck legs to a plate, increase the heat, and fry the potatoes and onions in batches until lightly golden, pouring off some of the fat if there is an excessive amount. Sprinkle generously with the thyme leaves and season well with salt and pepper.

Arrange the duck legs on top of the potatoes and onions, cover with a lid, and cook in the oven for about 1 hour or until the duck is cooked through and crisp, and the potatoes and onions are soft, juicy, and slightly caramelized. Check every now and then.

Serve the duck legs with the potatoes and onions along with the cooking juices, garnished with sprigs of fresh thyme.

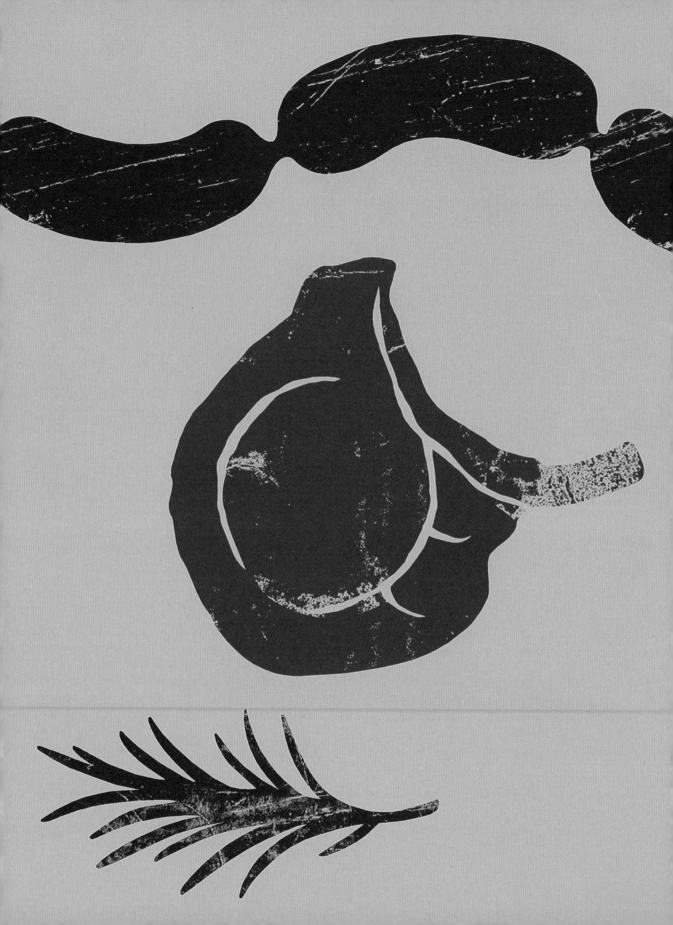

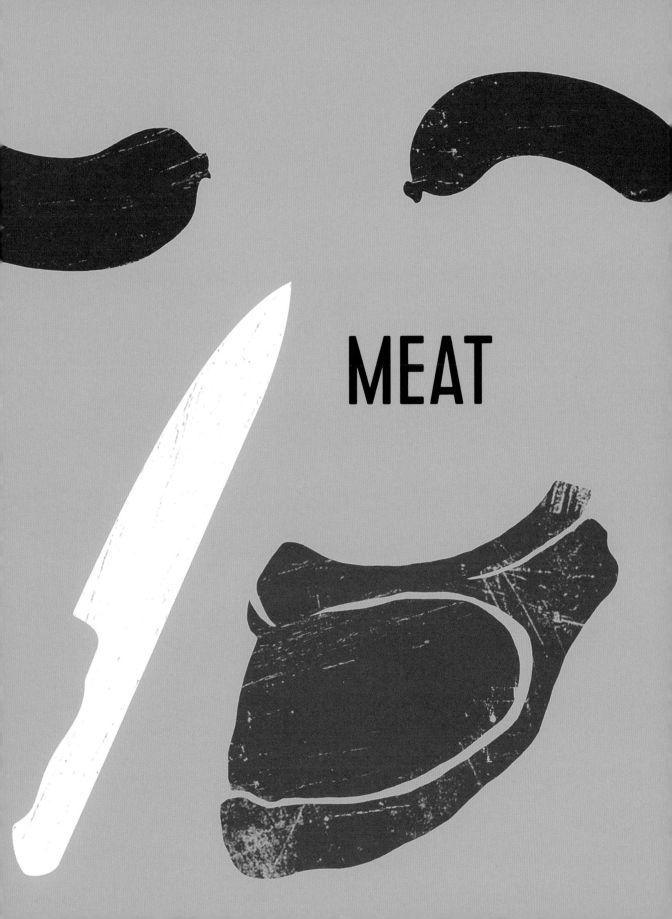

MEAT

The "eat less meat but better quality" message is really getting through. I love to serve slivers of beautiful, well-hung steak, over a salad of leaves. Here the Crozier Blue cheese crumbles add an irresistible salty note, a whole meal on a platter.

Chargrilled steak & *Crozier Blue salad*

- 2 well-hung sirloin steaks
- 1 large garlic clove, halved
- 1 tablespoon extra virgin olive oil, plus extra for drizzling
- ¼ teaspoon smoked paprika
- a pinch of cayenne pepper
- sea salt flakes and freshly ground black pepper, and a little sugar

FOR THE SALAD
- 12-15 ripe red and yellow cherry tomatoes
- 6 radishes
- 4 scallions, plus extra to garnish
- 1-2 Little Gem lettuce, cut into quarters or sixths
- ⅓-½ cucumber, halved lengthwise and sliced at an angle
- society garlic (*Tulbaghia violacea*) or chive blossoms, if available

FOR THE BLUE CHEESE DRESSING
- 3½ ounces Crozier Blue or dolcelatte
- scant 1 cup sour cream or buttermilk
- 2 tablespoons white wine vinegar
- 4 tablespoons heavy cream
- ½ teaspoon Dijon mustard
- 1-2 teaspoons honey

Score the fat of the steaks. Rub the surface of the steaks with the cut clove of garlic, then crush the garlic and mix with the extra virgin olive oil, smoked paprika, cayenne pepper, and some salt and black pepper. Dip both sides of the steaks into the spicy oil and allow to soak up the flavors while you make the blue cheese dressing.

To make the dressing, crumble the cheese into the cream (or buttermilk) and stir in the wine vinegar, Dijon mustard, and honey. Season to taste.

Heat a grill pan over high heat. Sear the steaks on both sides and continue to cook for 2–4 minutes on each side until medium rare. Turn onto the fat side and cook until it becomes crisp and delicious. You may have to hold it with tongs. Leave the steaks to rest while you prepare the salad.

Slice the tomatoes in half around the equator and others in quarters. Add to a bowl and season with salt and pepper and a little sugar. Slice or quarter the radishes, slice the scallions lengthwise at an angle, and add to the bowl, along with the cucumber. Drizzle with a little olive oil and toss. Arrange some of the outer leaves of the Little Gem on a plate, scatter the salad evenly over the platter.

Slice the steak into ¼-inch-thick slices and tuck them into the salad. Put a dollop of blue cheese dressing here and there or serve in a separate bowl on the side.

Sprinkle with sliced scallions and garnish with society garlic flowers or chive blossom, if available. Serve soon.

- 2 tablespoons extra virgin olive oil
- 18–25 ounces stewing meat (beef, veal, mutton or pork), cut into ½–¾-inch cubes
- 8 ounces onions, chopped (about 2 cups)
- 2–3 garlic cloves, crushed
- 1 green bell pepper, seeded and sliced
- 1¼ cups homemade beef stock or water
- 1 tablespoon tomato paste
- 1 teaspoon ground cumin
- 9 ounces (1½ cups) red kidney beans, cooked
- sea salt flakes and brown sugar

FOR THE COLORADO SAUCE
- 6–7 small dried chilies or 4–5 large fresh ones
- 1 large red bell pepper, seeded
- 1 large onion, chopped
- 1 large garlic clove, peeled
- sea salt
- 1 tablespoon chipotle chili in adobo sauce (optional)

FOR THE GUACAMOLE
- 1 ripe avocado (Hass if available)
- 1–2 tablespoons freshly squeezed lime juice
- 1 tablespoon extra virgin olive oil
- 1 tablespoon chopped cilantro or flat-leaf parsley
- freshly ground black pepper

FOR THE TOMATO & CILANTRO SALSA
- 4 very ripe tomatoes, chopped
- 1 tablespoon chopped red or white onion
- 1 garlic clove, crushed
- ½–1 red or green chili, such as Jalapeño or Serrano, seeded and finely chopped
- 1–2 tablespoons chopped cilantro
- a squeeze of organic lime juice
- sea salt flakes, freshly ground black pepper, and sugar

TO SERVE
- ½ cup sour cream
- 1¼ cups grated Cheddar cheese
- a generous handful of fresh cilantro leaves
- 36–40 tortilla chips

SERVES 6

Buy stewing meat for this dish, rather than the finest cuts, and try to avoid ground beef. Colorado sauce is a delicious sauce to use when making chili con carne, rather than chili powder. It is very versatile and can also be used as a marinade for grilled or barbecued meats.

Chili *con carne*

Start with the Colorado sauce. If the chilies are dried, soak them in a little water for an hour, then slit them and wash out the seeds. Discard the stalks and do the same with the red bell pepper. Puree all the sauce ingredients in a food processor, adding a little of the chili soaking water if necessary. If you are using fresh chilies, you might need to add a tablespoon or two of cold water. Season to taste with salt. Add the chipotle chili in adobo sauce, if using.

Heat a splash of extra virgin olive oil in a large casserole over high heat and brown the meat in batches. Remove to a plate. Add the onion, reduce the heat to medium, and fry for 4–5 minutes until soft and just beginning to color. Add the crushed garlic and continue to cook for a minute or two. Return the meat to the pan and add the green bell pepper and Colorado sauce. Pour in just enough stock or water to barely cover the ingredients. Cover the pan tightly with a lid and simmer gently over low heat for about 30 minutes, or until the meat is cooked and the sauce has reduced to a thick, brownish-red sauce. Check the liquid occasionally and if it seems to be reducing too quickly reduce the heat further and top up with water.

Add the tomato paste, cumin, and cooked kidney beans. Season with salt and brown sugar. Simmer for a further 15 minutes.

Meanwhile, make the guacamole. Scoop out the flesh from the avocado and mash it with a fork. Add the lime juice, olive oil, and chopped cilantro or parsley, and season to taste with black pepper. If you are not serving immediately, cover the surface with a layer of plastic wrap and chill until needed.

To make the tomato and cilantro salsa, mix all of the ingredients together and season to taste with salt, pepper, and sugar.

To serve, put a dollop of sour cream on top of the chili, sprinkle with the grated cheese, and garnish with some fresh cilantro. Accompany with the tortilla chips, guacamole, and tomato salsa.

This is super tasty, so a little goes a long way—but it's so worth using fresh lime leaves. I have several lime trees at home in large pots, which are becoming quite shrubby—the leaves freeze pretty well and a plant makes a brilliant gift for a friend who loves to cook.

Thai beef curry *with peanut sauce*

- generous 2½ cups coconut milk
- 1–3 tablespoons red curry paste
- 3 tablespoons fish sauce
- 2½ tablespoons palm sugar or brown sugar
- 2 stalks of fresh lemongrass, bruised
- 1 pound rump steak, cut into thin strips
- ½ cup roasted peanuts, finely chopped or pulsed in a food processor
- 1–2 red chilies, sliced
- 5 kaffir lime leaves, torn—fresh are best, but otherwise use dried
- sea salt flakes and freshly ground black pepper
- 10–15 Thai basil leaves (optional)

FOR THE THAI JASMINE RICE
- 12 ounces (scant 2 cups) Thai jasmine rice
- 1½ cups water

Start by cooking the sticky rice. Put the rice and water into a heavy-based saucepan and bring to a boil. Stir once and cover with a tight-fitting lid (if your lid isn't tight fitting, cover the pan first with parchment and then with the lid). Reduce the heat to the absolute minimum—use a heat diffuser mat, if you have one. Cook on the lowest possible heat for 15 minutes. Do not uncover during cooking. Remove the pan from the heat, keeping it covered, and set aside for 5 minutes before serving. The rice will stay warm for several hours if necessary.

To make the curry, pour half the coconut milk into a wok and cook over medium heat, stirring, until the milk boils and separates—it will look curdled, but don't worry. Whisk in the red curry paste and cook for 3–4 minutes until fragrant and aromatic. Add the fish sauce, palm sugar or brown sugar, and lemongrass. Continue to cook over gentle heat for a few minutes before adding the rest of the coconut milk. Bring back to a boil.

Add the strips of beef and the peanuts, stir, and cook gently for 6–7 minutes or until most of the liquid has evaporated. Be careful not to overcook the beef. If necessary, you can remove the meat with a slotted spoon after the allotted cooking time and return the pan to the heat to reduce the sauce further. Return the meat to the pan, if necessary, and throw in the chilies and lime leaves. Season to taste and remove the lemongrass.

Serve with the Thai fragrant rice, garnished with Thai basil leaves, if available.

This is a rich and delicious stew that just gets better and better. The flavor deepens when made the day before. Serve with polenta, tagliatelle, or some fluffy mashed potato and a tasty green salad, as you wish.

Beef & Agen prune stew

- 18 Agen mi-cuit or semisoft prunes, pitted
- 2 tablespoons extra virgin olive oil
- 14 ounces carrots, cut into ½-inch slices
- 10 ounces onions, sliced (about 2 cups)
- 3 pounds well-hung stewing beef or lean flank, trimmed of fat and cut into 1½-inch cubes
- 1 heaped tablespoon all-purpose flour
- scant ⅔ cup red wine
- scant ⅔ cup brown beef stock
- 1 x 14-ounce can of chopped tomatoes
- 8 medium potatoes, washed and peeled at the last minute
- 2 tablespoons chopped flat-leaf parsley
- sea salt flakes and freshly ground black pepper
- a good green salad and some polenta, tagliatelle, or mashed potatoes, to serve (optional)

Preheat the oven to 315°F.

Place the prunes in a bowl, cover with boiling water, and set aside to soak.

Heat 1 tablespoon olive oil in a 10-inch/3-quart casserole over gentle heat and cook the sliced carrots and onions for 10 minutes, covered, until soft. Remove from the pan and set aside on a plate.

Heat another tablespoon of olive oil in the casserole over medium heat until almost smoking. Add the pieces of beef and sear on all sides in the hot fat. Reduce the heat to low, stir in the flour, and cook for 1 minute. Pour in the wine, stock, and chopped tomatoes and bring slowly to a boil, stirring. Add the onions and carrots back to the pan and season with salt and pepper. Cover with a lid and simmer gently for 1¼ hours.

Arrange the whole peeled potatoes on top of the meat and vegetables and replace the lid. Return the casserole to the oven and continue to cook for a further 1 hour or until the meat is tender. Add the whole drained prunes and chopped parsley about 15 minutes before the end.

Serve with a green salad and some tagliatelle, polenta, or mashed potatoes, if you like.

The word tagine refers both to the distinctive earthenware cooking pot with its shallow base and conical top and to the multitude of stew-like dishes that are cooked in it. These can be based on meat, fish, poultry, or vegetables. In Morocco, tagine is eaten alone but I am including a recipe for plain couscous in case you'd enjoy it as an accompaniment.

Tagine of lamb *with preserved lemon*

- 3 pounds boned shoulder of lamb, trimmed of fat and cut into 1½-inch cubes
- scant 2 teaspoons ground cinnamon
- 1 teaspoon ground ginger
- 1 teaspoon freshly ground black pepper
- a generous pinch of saffron threads
- 1¼ cups raisins
- 3½ tablespoons butter
- 2 onions, chopped
- 2 garlic cloves, finely chopped
- salt
- 2 tablespoons honey
- 3 tablespoons chopped cilantro
- 1 small or ½ large preserved lemon, diced
- ⅔ cup toasted sliced almonds

FOR THE COUSCOUS
- 2 cups couscous
- 2 cups boiling water
- 4 tablespoons extra virgin olive oil
- sea salt flakes and freshly ground black pepper

TO SERVE
- cilantro sprigs and chopped mint (optional)
- plain yogurt

Combine the cinnamon, ginger, black pepper, and saffron with 4 tablespoons of water in a large bowl. Add the lamb and toss well to coat. If you have the time, you can marinate the lamb for up to 24 hours, covered, in the refrigerator. Place the raisins in a bowl, cover with water and set aside to plump up while you cook the lamb.

Melt the butter in a tagine or a large heavy-based frying pan with a lid. Add the lamb, onions, garlic, ½ teaspoon of salt, and enough water to come halfway up the meat. Bring up to a boil, cover the pan with a lid and reduce the heat to a gentle simmer. Cook for about an hour, turning the lamb occasionally until the meat is meltingly tender.

Add the drained raisins, honey, and half the fresh cilantro. Continue to cook for a further 30 minutes or so over gentle heat, uncovered, until the sauce is thick and unctuous. Season to taste.

While the tagine is cooking, scoop out the flesh from the preserved lemon and discard, then chop up the peel.

To make the couscous, put the couscous into a Pyrex bowl. Pour over the boiling water from the kettle, cover with the bowl with plastic wrap and set aside to soak for 15 minutes. Stir with a fork to break up the clumps, mix in the olive oil, and season with salt and pepper.

Sprinkle the preserved lemon, almonds, and the remaining cilantro over the lamb just before serving. Plain yogurt makes a delicious accompaniment. I also love to stir in some freshly chopped mint. There's no need to serve with any vegetables, but a green salad would be a delicious addition.

Bean stews make the perfect one-pot meal—
comforting, filling, and inexpensive. Gremolata
is a fresh-tasting mix of chopped parsley, garlic, and
lemon zest. I use it to sprinkle over roast or braised
meats, pastas, or anything pan-grilled—delicious! If
you're short of time, you could replace it with some
chopped parsley instead.

Slow-cooked lamb *with cannellini beans, tomatoes & rosemary*

- 18 ounces boned leg or shoulder of lamb, trimmed of fat and cut into 1¼-inch cubes
- all-purpose flour, for dusting
- 2 tablespoons extra virgin olive oil
- 2 ounces onions, finely chopped (about ½ cup)
- 2 garlic cloves, finely chopped
- 8 ounces carrots, finely diced (about 2 cups)
- 1 celery stalk, finely diced
- 2 bay leaves
- a few generous sprigs of rosemary
- 2 x 14-ounce cans of Italian chopped tomatoes
- 1½ cups white wine
- 1½ cups homemade lamb stock or water
- 2 x 14-ounce cans of cannellini beans, rinsed in cold water and drained
- sea salt flakes and freshly ground black pepper

FOR THE GREMOLATA
- 4 tablespoons chopped flat-leaf parsley
- 1 generous teaspoon grated or finely chopped organic lemon zest
- 2 garlic cloves, finely chopped
- sea salt flakes, to taste

Dust the cubes of lamb with flour and season with salt and pepper. Heat the olive oil in a casserole and fry the lamb in batches until brown. Remove the lamb to a plate and set aside.

Add the onions, garlic, carrots, and celery to the casserole and cook over medium heat for 3–4 minutes until the onions are beginning to soften and are slightly golden. Add the lamb.

Reduce the heat to low and put in the bay leaves, rosemary, tomatoes, white wine, and lamb stock or water. Bring slowly to a boil, cover the pan with a lid, and simmer very gently for about 1½ hours, or until the lamb is tender. Add the cannellini beans 15 minutes before the end.

To make the gremolata, mix all of the ingredients in a small bowl, season to taste with salt, and serve soon.

Remove the rosemary sprigs from the lamb and check the seasoning. Serve with the gremolata.

SERVES 8

This rich spicy dish is often better reheated the next day, or the day after. If you have any of the sauce left over, toss it with some pasta or noodles for a simple supper.

Masala lamb shanks

- 8 lamb shanks, weighing
  approx. 2 pounds 10 ounces in total
- 1 tablespoon ground turmeric
- 1¼-inch piece of fresh ginger, grated
- 3 garlic cloves, crushed
- 2 tablespoons extra virgin olive oil
- 1 bay leaf
- 1 cinnamon stick
- 5 cloves
- 6 cardamom pods, bashed
- 1 pound onions, sliced
- 1 x 14-ounce can of chopped tomatoes
- 1–2 teaspoons honey
- 2 teaspoons ground cumin
- 3 teaspoons ground coriander
- 2–3 green chilies, halved
- 1 x 14-ounce can of coconut milk
- 8 large potatoes, peeled and halved
- sea salt
- lots of fresh cilantro sprigs, to serve

FOR THE MASALA PASTE
- ⅓ cup dried shredded coconut
- 1½ tablespoons coriander seeds
- 1 tablespoon poppy seeds
- 1 tablespoon fennel seeds
- 1 tablespoon mustard seeds
- ½ tablespoon freshly ground
  black pepper
- 2–3 red chilies, finely chopped

FOR THE MINT YOGURT
- 4 tablespoons chopped mint
- 1⅓ cups plain yogurt
- sea salt and a little honey, to taste

Put the lamb shanks into an 11–11½-inch/4½–5-quart casserole and add the turmeric, ginger, garlic, and some salt. Pour in enough water to cover (approx. 2½ quarts) and bring slowly to a boil. Reduce the heat, cover with a lid, and simmer gently for 2 hours or until the meat is tender.

Meanwhile, grind the ingredients for the masala paste in a spice grinder or pestle and mortar, and set aside until needed.

Once the lamb shanks are cooked, remove them carefully from the pan and keep warm. Pour all of the cooking liquid into a separate pan and set aside.

Return the casserole to a low heat with the extra virgin olive oil. Add the bay leaf, cinnamon, cloves, and cardamom and stir-fry for 1–2 minutes. Add the onions and fry for 5–6 minutes until they start to soften. Add the chopped tomatoes and honey and cook for 5 minutes. Sprinkle in the ground cumin and coriander, add the green chilies, and cook for 3 minutes. Finally stir in the masala paste and coconut milk and bring slowly to a boil. Taste and add salt, if necessary.

Return the cooked lamb shanks to the pan and pour in enough of the cooking liquid to come halfway up the shanks. Bring to a boil, cover with a lid, and simmer gently for 10 minutes, turning the shanks several times during the cooking time.

Add the potatoes to the pan, replace the lid and cook for 20 minutes or until the potatoes are fully cooked and the lamb is almost falling off the bone. Season to taste.

To make the mint yogurt, stir the chopped mint into the yogurt and season to taste with salt and honey.

Sprinkle the casserole with lots of fresh cilantro and serve with the mint yogurt.

A substantial pot of stew fortified with pearl barley, this is really good with lots of gremolata sprinkled over the top. It is a variation of Irish stew, which is the quintessential one-pot dish—the recipe for the original Ballymaloe version can be found in my *Forgotten Skills of Cooking* book.

Lamb & pearl barley
stew & *fresh herb gremolata*

- 12-ounce piece of green (unsmoked) bacon (blanched if salty)
- 4 pounds gigot or rack chops from the shoulder of lamb, not less than 1 inch thick
- well-seasoned all-purpose flour, for dusting
- a little extra virgin olive oil, for frying
- 12 ounces mushrooms, thinly sliced
- 1 pound 9 ounces whole, small onions— baby ones are nicest
- 12 ounces carrots, peeled and thickly sliced
- 5½ ounces parsnips, peeled and thickly sliced
- scant 2¼ cups pearl barley
- approx. 3 quarts (12 cups) homemade lamb or chicken stock
- sprig of thyme
- sea salt flakes and freshly ground black pepper

FOR THE GREMOLATA
- 4 tablespoons chopped mixed herbs, such as flat-leaf parsley, chervil, and mint
- 2 garlic cloves, finely chopped
- 1 generous teaspoon grated or finely chopped organic lemon zest
- sea salt flakes, to taste

Preheat the oven to 350°F.

First make the stew. Cut the rind off the bacon (if necessary) and cut into approx. ½-inch cubes. Divide the lamb into 8 pieces and roll in the well-seasoned flour.

Heat a little oil in a 10-inch/3-quart casserole over medium heat and sauté the bacon until crisp. Remove to a plate. Sauté the mushrooms, season well, and set aside. Add the lamb to the casserole in batches, with a little more olive oil if necessary, and sauté until golden. Heat control is crucial here: the pan mustn't burn, yet it must be hot enough to sauté the lamb. If the pan is too cool, the lamb will stew rather than sauté and as a result the meat may be tough. Remove the lamb to a plate. Add another splash of olive oil to the pan and sauté the onions, carrots, and parsnips until golden. Return the bacon and lamb to the casserole, together with the pearl barley. Season well, pour in the stock, add the thyme, and bring to a simmer. Cover with a lid and transfer to the oven for 1–1¼ hours until meltingly tender; the cooking time will depend on the age of the lamb and how long it was sautéed for. Add the mushrooms about 30 minutes before the end.

Meanwhile, make the gremolata. Mix together the chopped herbs and garlic in a small bowl, add the lemon zest, and season to taste with a little salt.

Once the casserole is cooked, remove the thyme and season to taste. Leave the casserole to sit for 15–30 minutes to allow the pearl barley to swell. (If necessary, the casserole can be reheated later in the day, or the next day.) Serve bubbling hot, sprinkled with the gremolata.

SERVES 4-6

This delicious Greek-inspired lamb, squash, and orzo stew is tender, rich, and sweet—a perfect one-pot winter supper. You can increase the quantity of orzo to 8 ounces if you wish, but I like the proportion as it is.

Lamb, *butternut squash* & *orzo* stew

- 2 tablespoons extra virgin olive oil
- 7 ounces onions, sliced (about 1⅓ cups)
- 1 x 2–3-inch cinnamon stick
- 1 tablespoon chopped marjoram
- 2 sprigs of fresh thyme
- 2¼ pounds organic boned shoulder of lamb, trimmed of fat and cut into roughly 1½-inch cubes
- 1 x 14-ounce can of plum tomatoes, roughly chopped
- 2½ cups homemade lamb or chicken stock
- 14 ounces butternut squash, peeled and cut into 1-inch cubes
- 7 ounces (about 1 cup) orzo
- 2 tablespoons grated Parmesan cheese
- 2 tablespoons chopped flat-leaf parsley
- zest of ½ organic lemon
- sea salt flakes and freshly ground black pepper

FOR THE MINTED YOGURT

- 1 cup Greek or thick plain yogurt
- 2 tablespoons chopped mint leaves
- 1 teaspoon freshly squeezed organic lemon juice

Preheat the oven to 315°F.

Heat the olive oil in a large 9½-inch/4-quart casserole over medium heat. Add the onions, cinnamon stick, marjoram and thyme and cook for 4-5 minutes until the onions start to soften. Fry the lamb in batches until lightly browned, and then season with plenty of salt and pepper. Add the chopped tomatoes and their juice and pour in about 2 cups of the stock. Bring to a boil, and then cover the pan with a lid and transfer to the oven for about 1 hour. Remove the pan from the oven, stir in the squash, and season again. Replace the lid and return to the oven for a further 20 minutes. Stir in the orzo and cook on the stovetop or return to the oven for a further 20 minutes. Degrease if necessary with a spoon.

To make the minted yogurt, mix together the yogurt, mint, and lemon juice in a small bowl.

Sprinkle the stew with the Parmesan, chopped parsley and lemon zest and serve immediately with the minted yogurt.

So named because traditionally in France local people would have brought their cassoulet, gratins, and roasts to be cooked in the residual heat of the baker's wood-burning oven after he had finished baking the bread—hence the name *à la boulangère*. Nothing could be simpler: slide a roasting pan of boulangère potatoes into the oven, sit a leg of lamb on a rack above and, as the lamb cooks, its delicious juices drip onto the potatoes to enrich the dish further.

Lamb *à la boulangère*

- approx. 6½ pounds organic leg of lamb
- 6½ pounds potatoes
- 3½ tablespoons butter
- 3 large onions, thinly sliced
- 1 tablespoon thyme leaves
- 3½ cups hot homemade lamb or chicken stock
- sea salt flakes and freshly ground black pepper
- green salad, to serve

Preheat the oven to 350°F.

Season the leg of lamb with salt and pepper. If it's a big leg, and you suspect it may take longer than an hour to cook, pop it on a rack in the preheated oven while you prepare the potatoes (have a container not far beneath to catch the juices). Prepare the potatoes by peeling them and cutting them into slices about ¼ inch thick.

Butter a roasting pan approx. 13 x 9 inches and arrange the potatoes in alternating layers with the sliced onions and a sprinkling of thyme leaves. Season each layer with salt and pepper. Arrange the top layer of potatoes in overlapping slices. Pour in the hot stock and dot with the remaining butter.

Slide the pan into the oven, right under the rack with the leg of lamb cooking on it so that the juices drip down. Bake for 1–1½ hours or until the potatoes are cooked and the top is golden brown and crusty. Carve the lamb in thick slices and serve with a generous helping of boulangère potatoes and a good green salad.

A shoulder of pork is the best cut to use for this long, slow cooking method, as the meat is layered with fat which slowly melts away. Try to find a traditional breed. Slow-cooked shoulder of pork can be served in so many ways with so many accompaniments, but I love it as a filler for tacos along with all the toppings.

Pork taco *party*

- 1 x 6–7-pound whole shoulder of organic, free-range pork, skin on
- 8 garlic cloves, peeled
- 4 tablespoons fennel seeds
- sea salt flakes and freshly ground black pepper
- 1 teaspoon chili flakes (optional)
- 2 teaspoons thyme leaves

TO SERVE
- 16–20 soft corn tortillas—have a few extra on hand depending on how ravenous people are
- guacamole (page 65) or slices of avocado
- tomato salsa (page 65)
- hot sauce
- 6–8 scallions, cut on the diagonal
- 8–10 tablespoons cilantro leaves
- 3 organic limes, halved, for squeezing

Preheat the oven to 350°F.

Using a small sharp knife or, better still, a Stanley knife, score the rind of the pork with deep cuts about ¼ inch apart.

Crush the garlic with the fennel seeds in a pestle and mortar and mix in some salt and pepper and a few chili flakes (if using). Sprinkle over the pork, rubbing it into the cuts, over the rind and all over the surface of the meat.

Place the shoulder of pork on a rack in an approx. 13 x 12-inch roasting pan and roast for 30 minutes or until the skin begins to blister and brown. Reduce the temperature to 250°F and continue to roast for 5–6 hours until the meat is completely soft under the crisp skin. By this time, the meat should give way and almost fall off the bone. Pour off the delicious pork fat from time to time and save it in jars for roasting or sautéing potatoes another day.

Lift the crisp skin off the slow-cooked pork, chop and keep warm. Lift the pork off the bones and shred into a large serving bowl.

Strain the pork pan juices into a large measuring cup and pour off and discard all the fat from the surface. Add the rich juices to the pork. Season the meat with salt and pepper, a few chili flakes, and some thyme leaves. Keep hot.

Lay out the accompaniments on the table: a pile of soft corn tortillas, a bowl of guacamole or sliced avocado, some tomato salsa, a bottle of hot sauce, some slivered scallions, and fresh cilantro. Bring the hot meat and cracklings to the table and allow everyone to help themselves.

A gorgeous pot of bean stew, so warm and comforting for a late fall or winter supper. Use your favorite juicy pork sausages.

Sausage, haricot or flageolet beans *with tomato & rosemary*

- 8 ounces (about 1¼ cups) dried haricot (navy), cannellini, or flageolet beans (or 2 x 14-ounce cans of cooked beans)
- bouquet garni
- 1 carrot, peeled
- 1 onion, peeled
- 3 tablespoons extra virgin olive oil, plus extra for frying
- 1 pound fennel and chili pork sausages
- 6 ounces (1½ cups) chopped onion
- 4 large garlic cloves, crushed
- 14-ounce can of plum tomatoes, chopped
- 1 tablespoon chopped rosemary
- sea salt flakes, freshly ground black pepper, and sugar
- flat-leaf parsley or chervil, to serve

Variations

CHEESY SAUSAGE, HARICOT OR FLAGEOLET BEANS WITH TOMATO & ROSEMARY

Spoon the finished stew into a shallow baking dish and scatter over 1 cup breadcrumbs mixed with 1¾ tablespoons butter and ½ cup grated Cheddar cheese. Flash under the broiler until crisp and golden on top.

HARICOT OR FLAGEOLET BEANS WITH TOMATO & ROSEMARY WITH CHORIZO OR 'NDUJA

Omit the sausages and add 4½ ounces 'nduja or sliced chorizo to the tomato base with the beans and rosemary.

Soak the beans overnight in a large pan with plenty of cold water. Next day, strain the beans, discarding the soaking liquid, and return them to the pan. Cover with fresh cold water and add the bouquet garni, whole carrot, and whole onion. Cover the pan with a lid and simmer for 30 minutes–1 hour until the beans are soft, but not mushy. Just before the end of cooking, season with salt. Remove the bouquet garni and vegetables from the pan and discard. Drain the beans, reserving the cooking liquid.

Fry the sausages in a few drops of oil over medium heat until nicely colored, then remove from the pan and set aside.

Heat the oil over lowish heat in the same saucepan and cook the chopped onion for 7–8 minutes until soft but not colored. Add the garlic and cook for a further minute or two before adding the chopped tomatoes and their juice, the cooked beans, and the rosemary. Add the sausages and simmer for 5–6 minutes, adding some of the bean liquid if the sauce starts to dry out. Season well with salt, freshly ground black pepper, and sugar. Cook for a further 5–6 minutes or until the sausages are heated through. The mixture should be juicy, but not swimming in liquid—if it starts to dry out, add more of the bean liquid.

To serve, scatter with plenty of parsley and accompany with a salad of organic leaves or crusty bread, if you wish.

Another perennial favorite, served here with orzo—a form of pasta that looks much like grains of rice. Pork fillet is sometimes referred to as pork steak or pork tenderloin. Chicken breast works brilliantly here also and the whole dish reheats perfectly.

Fillet of pork *with mushroom, rosemary & ginger*

- 2 x 18-ounce organic, free-range pork fillets
- 2 tablespoons butter
- 1 teaspoon chopped rosemary
- 2 tablespoons chopped shallot or scallion
- 3¾ ounces chanterelle mushrooms, roughly chopped (or thinly sliced flat mushrooms if chanterelles are not available)
- 2½ cups homemade chicken stock
- 1–2 teaspoons grated fresh ginger
- scant ⅔ cup heavy cream
- 7 ounces (about 1 cup) orzo
- sea salt flakes and freshly ground black pepper
- sprigs of fresh rosemary and rosemary flowers if in season, to garnish

Trim the pork fillet of all fat and membrane. Cut into slices ¾ inch thick.

Heat half of the butter in an 8½-inch sauté pan until foaming, put in the pork and turn it in the butter—do not let it brown. Add the chopped rosemary and toss to coat. Cover the pan with a round of wax paper and the lid, and cook over gentle heat for 5–7 minutes or until the pork is barely cooked. Remove the meat and juices to a plate.

Melt the remaining butter in the same pan over lowish heat and sweat the shallots very gently for 4-5 minutes until soft. Increase the heat, add the mushrooms and season with salt and pepper. Cook for 3–4 minutes until limp and fully cooked, and then remove the mushrooms to the plate with the pork (be careful not to overcook, or the lean pork will be dry).

Pour the chicken stock into the pan and add the ginger and cream. Bring to a boil, add ½ teaspoon of salt and stir in the orzo. Cover the pan with a lid and cook for 8 minutes with the lid on, and then 2 minutes with the lid off.

Add the pork and mushrooms back to the pan, adjust the seasoning and heat through for 2 minutes. Serve immediately, garnished with the fresh rosemary.

Based on a simple batter, this savory equivalent of
the French dessert clafoutis can be whipped up in
minutes. Here I use regular sausages, but I also love
to use spicy varieties, such as merguez or chorizo.
A little grainy mustard adds extra oomph.

Toad in the hole *with lots of fresh herbs*

- 1 pound homemade sausages or spicy
  sausages, such as merguez or chorizo
- 1–2 tablespoons extra virgin olive oil
- 1–2 tablespoons coarsely chopped
  flat-leaf parsley, to serve

FOR THE BATTER
- 1¾ cups all-purpose flour
- 4 organic, free-range eggs
- 2½ cups whole milk
- 2 tablespoons butter, melted
- 1 teaspoon Dijon mustard (optional)
- 4 tablespoons mixed chopped herbs,
  such as flat-leaf parsley, thyme, chives,
  and marjoram
- ½–1 teaspoon sea salt flakes and plenty
  of freshly ground black pepper

Preheat the oven to 450°F.

To make the batter, sift the flour into a bowl, make a well in the
center and crack in the lightly beaten eggs. Using a small whisk
or wooden spoon and stirring continuously, gradually draw in
the flour from the sides, adding the milk in a steady stream at
the same time. Once all the flour has been incorporated, whisk
in the remaining milk and the cooled melted butter, along with
the mustard (if using) and the herbs. Season with salt and
pepper. Set aside to rest while you cook the sausages.

Heat a little extra virgin olive oil in a 9 x 16-inch roasting pan,
1½ inches deep, add the sausages, and cook until golden on
all sides.

Pour the batter over the sausages and bake for 20–25 minutes
until the batter is well risen and crisp. Sprinkle with chopped
fresh parsley and serve.

Variation

TOAD IN THE HOLE WITH JAM & CREAM
For a quick sweet bite, make the batter as
above and cook in individual patty pans
or muffin pans. Top each with a dollop
of jam and softly whipped cream in the
center, and dust with powdered sugar,
to serve.

The flavor of this stew really improves if you cook it the day before and reheat it the next day—as well as improving the flavor, cooking the venison in advance ensures that it is meltingly tender. If needs must, and you are racing against the clock, just mix all the ingredients in the casserole, bring to a boil, and simmer until cooked. Baked potatoes work brilliantly with venison stew, but a layer of potatoes on top provides a wonderfully comforting meal in one pot. Scatter lots of fresh parsley over the potatoes before tucking in.

Venison & parsnip stew

- 3-pound shoulder of venison, trimmed and cut into 1½-inch cubes
- ⅓ cup all-purpose flour, for dusting
- 2 tablespoons extra virgin olive oil
- 8-ounce piece of fatty salted pork or green (unsmoked) streaky bacon, cut into 1½-inch cubes
- 2 large onions, chopped
- 1 large carrot, diced
- 2 large parsnips, diced
- 1 large garlic clove, crushed
- 2 cups homemade beef stock
- bouquet garni
- 8–12 medium potatoes
- a squeeze of organic lemon juice
- sea salt flakes and freshly ground black pepper

FOR THE MARINADE
- 1¼–1½ cups gutsy red wine
- 1 medium onion, sliced
- 3 tablespoons brandy
- 3 tablespoons extra virgin olive oil
- bouquet garni
- horseradish sauce (optional)

TO SERVE
- lots of chopped flat-leaf parsley
- green vegetables, such as Brussels sprouts, calabrese, or cabbage

First marinate the meat. Season the cubes of venison with salt and pepper. Combine all of the ingredients for the marinade in a large bowl, add the venison, and set aside to marinate for at least 1 hour, or better still overnight.

Preheat the oven to 300°F.

Drain the meat, reserving the marinade, and pat dry with paper towels. Tip the flour onto a plate and season well. Turn the cubes of venison in the seasoned flour to coat on all sides.

Heat the oil in a 10-inch/3-quart casserole pan over low heat, add the salted pork or bacon and cook for 4–5 minutes, stirring, until it starts to release its fat. Increase the heat to medium and fry the salted pork or bacon until golden brown. Transfer to a plate and set aside.

Add the venison to the casserole in batches and fry over medium heat until nicely colored on all sides. Avoid the temptation to increase the temperature or the fat will burn. Remove and set the batch aside while you color the rest.

Toss the vegetables in the casserole, stir in the garlic and then add the pork or bacon and venison.

Pour off any surplus fat from the casserole and remove the meat and vegetables and set aside. Deglaze the casserole by pouring in the strained marinade. Bring to a boil, stirring to dissolve the crusty bits on the base, add the pork or bacon and vegetables back in. →

Pour over enough stock to cover the meat and vegetables, and put in the bouquet garni. Bring the casserole to a gentle simmer on the stovetop, then cover with a lid and transfer to the oven for 1½ hours.

Remove the casserole from the oven and cover the surface of the stew with the whole potatoes. Season with salt and pepper. Cover the potatoes with a circle of wax paper, and then replace the lid. Return the casserole to the oven and cook for a further 1 hour or until both the venison and potatoes are cooked.

Season to taste. As well as adding salt and pepper, I find it often needs a bit of acidity in the form of lemon juice or crab apple jelly, if available.

Scatter with lots of freshly chopped parsley and serve with a nice big dish of Brussels sprouts, calabrese, or cabbage, and some homemade horseradish sauce.

I love this combination; in fact, I'm rather addicted to the Irish smoked black pudding (blood sausage) made in the traditional way with fresh blood and natural casings. The texture is soft and crumbly and delicious.

Smoked blood sausage *with* *charred onions & Jerusalem artichokes*

- 4 medium onions, peeled
- extra virgin olive oil, for drizzling
- 6–8 medium Jerusalem artichokes, scrubbed really well
- 7-ounce piece of smoked blood sausage or regular blood sausage, skin removed and cut into 16 pieces
- 8 sprigs of watercress
- 1 teaspoon Forum Chardonnay vinegar or good-quality white wine vinegar
- sea salt flakes and freshly ground black pepper

FOR THE APPLE & HORSERADISH SAUCE
- 1 cup applesauce
- ½ cup heavy cream
- 3 teaspoons grated fresh horseradish

Preheat the oven to 500°F.

Halve the onions and brush the cut side with extra virgin olive oil. Season with salt and pepper, and arrange on an approx. 16 x 17-inch baking sheet lined with parchment paper.

Slice the artichokes into ⅓-inch rounds and place in a bowl. Drizzle over 1 tablespoon olive oil, season well with salt and pepper, and arrange in a single layer around the onions.

Roast for 30–35 minutes until the vegetables are cooked and well colored.

Place the pieces of blood sausage in the same bowl, drizzle over 2 teaspoons of olive oil, and toss well to coat. Arrange the blood sausage over the roasted vegetables and roast for a further 3–4 minutes until colored.

To make the sauce, combine the applesauce and cream in a small pan, bring to a boil, and stir in the horseradish.

Place the sprigs of watercress in a bowl and drizzle with the vinegar and 3 teaspoons of extra virgin olive oil. Toss well to coat.

To serve, divide the dressed watercress between eight plates and arrange half an onion and two pieces of blood sausage on each. Scatter with the artichokes and dollop the sauce here and there.

FISH & SEAFOOD

Pronounced "poh-kay", this Hawaiian version of sashimi or ceviche is often made with really fresh raw tuna. Raw mackerel is also delicious.

Mackerel poke

- 8 super-fresh mackerel fillets or 1¾ pounds fresh tuna, cut into ¾-inch chunks
- 1 small cucumber, cut into ½-inch dice
- 2 avocados, pitted, peeled, and cut into 1-inch cubes
- 8 scallions, sliced on the diagonal
- 1 tablespoon each of toasted black and white sesame seeds
- 1–2 sheets of nori, snipped into strips
- cilantro leaves, to garnish

FOR THE SUSHI RICE
- 1 pound (scant 2½ cups) sushi rice "No 1 Extra Fancy" or other premium grade
- 2½ cups cold water

FOR THE VINEGAR WATER
- 3½ tablespoons rice wine vinegar
- 1½ tablespoons sugar
- 2½ teaspoons salt

FOR THE MIRIN DRESSING
- 2 tablespoons rice wine vinegar
- 4 teaspoons sesame oil
- 1 tablespoon mirin
- 2 tablespoons soy sauce
- juice of 2 organic limes

First prepare the sushi rice. Rinse the rice for 10 minutes in a colander or strainer under cold running water or until the water becomes clear. Tip the rice into a heavy-based saucepan, cover with the 2½ cups of cold water and set aside for 30–45 minutes to "wake up the rice."

Bring the rice to a boil and simmer for 10 minutes until all of the water has been absorbed. Avoid the temptation to stir the rice or remove the lid. Increase the heat right at the end for the last 10 seconds, just before you turn off the heat. Remove the lid, place a dish towel over the rice and replace the lid. Set aside for 20 minutes.

To make the vinegar water, combine the rice wine vinegar, sugar, and salt in a medium bowl and stir until the sugar and salt have dissolved. Scoop out the rice into a flat earthenware bowl. While the rice is still hot, pour the vinegar solution over the rice and mix together in a slicing action with the aid of a straight-ended wooden spoon. Do not stir. You must do this quickly, preferably cooling the rice with a fan—which is much easier to do if you have a helper. Leave the rice to cool, covered with paper towels or a dish towel to soak up any excess moisture as it cools.

To make the mirin dressing, whisk the rice wine vinegar, sesame oil, mirin, soy sauce, and freshly squeezed lime juice in a medium bowl. Add the mackerel (or tuna) and turn in the dressing. Add the diced cucumber and cubed avocado and toss gently together.

Divide the cooled rice between shallow bowls and top with the mackerel mixture. Sprinkle with the scallions, sesame seeds, and some shards of nori, and garnish with fresh cilantro leaves. Drizzle any remaining dressing over the top and serve right away.

There are always gasps of appreciation when I bring a pot of this fish stew to the table. If you don't have Serrano ham, use a little diced chorizo or 'nduja. Provide lots of crusty sourdough to mop up all the juices.

Andalusian shellfish stew

- ½ teaspoon saffron strands
- 2½ cups homemade chicken stock
- approx. 6 tablespoons extra virgin olive oil
- 2 onions, chopped
- 2 garlic cloves, crushed
- 1 large red bell pepper, seeded and sliced
- 1 large green bell pepper, seeded and sliced
- 6–12 waxy potatoes, cut into 1-inch dice
- 3¾-ounce piece of Serrano ham, cut into ½-inch dice
- 1 x 14-ounce can of lima beans or cannellini beans*
- 4 pounds cockles or mussels, or a mixture, scrubbed and washed really well
- sea salt flakes and freshly ground black pepper

TO SERVE
- 4–6 ripe tomatoes, peeled and very finely chopped
- sprigs of flat-leaf parsley

Put the saffron into a little bowl and cover with 2–3 tablespoons of chicken stock. Set aside to infuse.

Heat the olive oil in a 10-inch sauté pan over gentle heat and sweat the onions and garlic for 4–5 minutes until soft and slightly colored. Add the sliced peppers, season with salt and pepper, and continue to cook over medium heat for 6–8 minutes until the peppers are beginning to soften.

Add the diced potato, Serrano ham, and lima beans and pour in the chicken stock and saffron-infused stock. Bring to a boil and season to taste. Reduce the heat and simmer for about 10 minutes until the potatoes are cooked. The stew can be prepared to this point ahead of time.

Just before you are about to serve, return the pan to the heat and tip in the cockles or mussels. Cover with a lid. They will open in the heat. Cook for 2–4 minutes. Taste the sauce and season with salt and pepper.

Serve in deep soup bowls, topped with finely chopped fresh tomato and parsley. Accompany with crusty sourdough bread to mop up the juices.

* Alternatively, soak 7¾ ounces dried lima or cannellini beans in cold water overnight. Next day, pour off the soaking liquid and return the beans to the pan with a bouquet garni, a chunk of onion, and a few chunks of carrot. Cover with fresh water, bring to a boil and simmer for 30–45 minutes until just tender. Drain, remove the bouquet garni and flavorings, and continue as above.

SERVES 4

Who doesn't love these South Indian flavors? Mahi-mahi, a type of tuna, is the preferred fish for this dish in Kerala, but monkfish works brilliantly too. In India it is usual to have lots of "gravy," or sauce, to flavor the rice deliciously—and a relatively small serving of fish by our standards. If you can't find fresh curry leaves, use dried ones instead—but do keep an eye out for fresh leaves. When you find them, buy more than you need and freeze the surplus. Frozen curry leaves taste altogether better than dried. This curry base reheats extremely well, but don't cook the monkfish and rice until the last minute.

Keralan fish curry

- 1½ ounces dry tamarind
- 2 ounces coconut oil
- 3 tablespoons chopped shallot
- 1½ tablespoons grated fresh ginger
- 3 green chilies, split lengthwise
- 4½ ounces (scant ¾ cup) basmati rice
- 1 teaspoon black mustard seeds
- 1 tablespoon fresh curry leaves
- 1 teaspoon ground turmeric
- 1½ teaspoons sugar
- ¾–1 teaspoon chili powder
- 1½ teaspoons ground coriander
- 3½ cups fresh coconut milk
  or 2 x 14-ounce cans of coconut milk
- 1 pound 5 ounces monkfish (prepared
  weight), cut into 2-inch pieces
- 3½–7 tablespoons boiling water
  or homemade fish stock
- juice of ½–1 organic lime
- sea salt flakes, to taste

To prepare the tamarind water, place the tamarind in a small Pyrex bowl, cover with 5 tablespoons of boiling water and set aside to soak for 30 minutes to 1 hour. (Make sure the water covers the tamarind completely.) Strain through a fine sieve, discarding the pips and reserving the strained tamarind water.

Heat the coconut oil in a 10-inch sauté pan over low heat and gently fry the shallots, ginger, and green chilies for 5 minutes until they start to color.

Stir in the rice, mustard seeds, curry leaves, turmeric, sugar, chili powder, and coriander and cook for 2 minutes, stirring, taking care not to burn the spices or they will become bitter.

Add the coconut milk and tamarind water and season to taste with salt. Bring to a boil, cover with a lid, and simmer for 4 minutes.

Carefully tuck the pieces of monkfish into the pan, cover, and cook for 5–6 minutes until the rice and monkfish are both beautifully cooked. Remove the pan from the heat and set aside, still tightly covered with the lid, for 5–10 minutes. If you feel that the rice has soaked up too much of the sauce, add 3½–7 tablespoons of boiling water or fish stock to loosen the texture. Squeeze in the lime juice and season to taste. Serve with a salad of organic leaves, if you wish.

A gorgeous light fish stew, this dish is perfect for a dinner party. I love it with little aioli crostini, but of course you could serve it with some rice, orzo, or pasta.

Mediterranean shellfish stew *with aioli crostini*

- 3 tablespoons extra virgin olive oil
- 1 onion, sliced
- 3 garlic cloves, sliced
- 1 small red chili, seeded and chopped
- scant ⅔ cup dry white wine
- 1 pound 9 ounces ripe, peeled tomatoes, chopped or 1 x 14-ounce can of tomatoes and 4 fresh tomatoes, chopped
- 12 mussels, cleaned and debearded
- 12 clams or cockles, cleaned and debearded
- 12 raw Dublin Bay shrimp or langoustine, peeled
- 12 scallops, cut in half, or 12 collops of monkfish, ¾ inch thick (or a mixture)
- 1 tablespoon chopped chives
- 2 tablespoons chopped flat-leaf parsley
- 1 tablespoon chopped chervil
- sea salt flakes and freshly ground black pepper
- 4–6 slices of baguette, ¼ inch thick, to serve

FOR THE AIOLI
- 2 organic, free-range egg yolks
- 1–2 garlic cloves
- a pinch of English mustard or ¼ teaspoon Dijon mustard
- ¼ teaspoon sea salt flakes
- 2 teaspoons white wine vinegar
- 1 cup oil, such as sunflower, peanut, or olive oil, or a mixture (I use ¾ cup peanut oil and ¼ cup olive oil)
- 2 teaspoons chopped flat-leaf parsley

Heat the olive oil in a 10-inch/3-quart casserole over medium heat and cook the onion, garlic, and chili until soft but not colored. Add the wine and boil for 3–4 minutes, then add the tomatoes, reduce the heat to low, and cook for 25 minutes.

Meanwhile, make the aioli. Put the egg yolks into a bowl with the garlic, mustard, salt, and vinegar. Pour the oil(s) into a large measuring cup. Taking a whisk in one hand and the oil in the other, carefully drip the oil onto the egg yolks, drop by drop, whisking at the same time. Within a minute, you will notice that the mixture is beginning to thicken. When this happens, you can add the oil a little faster—but don't get too cheeky or it will suddenly curdle because the egg yolks can only absorb the oil at a certain pace.* Once all of the oil has been incorporated, beat in the parsley. Taste and add a little more seasoning and vinegar, if necessary.

Add the mussels and clams or cockles to the pan and cook for 1–2 minutes before adding the shrimp and scallops or monkfish. Cover with a lid and cook for about 4 minutes or until the mussels and clams are wide open and the shrimp and scallops or monkfish are opaque. Discard any shells that haven't opened.

Toast the bread for the crostini and top with a dollop of aioli. Keep the remainder covered in the refrigerator for 7–10 days.

Season the stew to taste and sprinkle with the herbs. Serve with the aioli crostini.

*Good to know
If the aioli curdles, it will suddenly become quite thin. If this happens you can quite easily remedy the situation by cracking another egg yolk into a clean bowl and whisking in the curdled aioli, half a teaspoon at a time.

A sublime way to cook beautiful fresh scallops, the ginger and chervil butter enhances the sweetness of the shellfish. You could cook the scallops in a gratin dish, but it's nicer to leave them in the scallop shells. I also like to add a teaspoon of smoked paprika instead or just use fresh thyme leaves.

Roast scallops *with* ginger & chervil butter

- 8 large scallops on the rounded half shell, if available
- 2-inch piece of fresh ginger, finely grated
- 1 teaspoon finely chopped chervil and thyme leaves
- 2 tablespoons softened butter
- 3 tablespoons extra virgin olive oil
- sea salt flakes and freshly ground black pepper
- organic lemon wedges, to serve

Preheat the oven to 500°F.

If the scallops are live, open the shell and remove the fringe and everything except the coral and muscle. Wash well. Put the scallops back into the rounded half shells and arrange on a baking sheet.

Combine the ginger, chopped chervil or thyme, softened butter, and extra virgin olive oil in a small bowl. Spoon a teaspoon of the herby butter onto each scallop and season with a little salt and pepper.

Bake in the very hot oven for 4–5 minutes until the butter is sizzling and the scallops are barely cooked. (A very hot broiler works also.) Serve immediately, accompanied by the lemon wedges and some crusty bread to mop up every drop of the delicious juices.

Variation

SCALLOPS WITH SMOKED PAPRIKA & ESPELETTE PEPPER
Substitute smoked paprika for ginger, chervil, or thyme in the butter. Slice each scallop into three rounds, arrange 6 rounds, slightly overlapping, in each shell. Put a couple of teaspoons of paprika butter on top, pop under a broiler, cook for 4–5 minutes or until the butter is sizzling, sprinkle with a few flakes of Espelette (or Aleppo) pepper and garnish with a sprig of chervil. Alternatively cook in an 8¼ x 11½-inch gratin dish.

Gray mullet, sea bass, monkfish, trout, or salmon are all quite delicious served in this way. Each person should have the special delight of opening their own bundle with its tantalizing aroma. A little hollandaise sauce, which can be made while the fish is cooking, turns this into a feast.

Fish in paper bundles
with cucumber & dill

- 4 x 3¾-ounce pieces of trout, wild salmon, gray sea mullet, sea bass, or monkfish, skinned
- 2 tablespoons chopped dill
- 3½ tablespoons butter
- ½ cucumber, thinly sliced
- sea salt flakes and freshly ground black pepper

Variation

SALMON WITH ZUCCHINI & GINGER & CHERVIL BUTTER

Take 4 x 3¼-ounce pieces of wild salmon and sprinkle all over with salt; set aside for 10 minutes. To make the ginger and chervil butter, cream 3½ tablespoons softened butter with 2 teaspoons of chopped chervil, ½ teaspoon of grated fresh ginger, a good squeeze of organic lemon juice, and a little black pepper. Grease the parchment paper with butter, as before. Slice 4¼ ounces zucchini very thinly and arrange half over the buttered side of the parchment paper. Lay the pieces of fish on top and cover with more overlapping slices of zucchini. Top with a spoonful of the chervil butter and proceed as above.

Preheat the oven to 350°F.

Salt the fish on both sides and set aside for 10 minutes, if possible. Dip both sides of the fish in the chopped dill.

Fold four pieces of parchment paper measuring approx. 12 x 10 inches in half and smear one half of each piece with a little butter.

Arrange the pieces of fish on the buttered side of the paper. Top each piece of fish with overlapping slices of cucumber and season with freshly ground pepper. Place a small pat of butter on top of the cucumber slices.

Fold the paper over the fish and wrap tightly to seal the edges. Put these bundles on a baking sheet. Cook for 6–10 minutes until the fish is just cooked through. Serve immediately.

A master recipe which we use for almost any round fish, such as cod, pollock, ling, haddock, or gray mullet. This perfect one-pot dish can be cooked ahead and reheated—just make sure there's lots of cheese sauce, otherwise it'll be dry and uninteresting instead of juicy and unctuous. Mussels, periwinkles, or shrimp can be added to make for a more elaborate and expensive version. Buttered leeks, peperonata, sautéed mushrooms, or tomato fondue are other options—simply put a tablespoon or two either on top of the fish or underneath it in the dish.

Cod, hake, or haddock
with dill & pangrattato

- 2½ pounds cod, hake, haddock, or gray mullet fillets
- 2 bay leaves
- 1 tablespoon butter
- 2½ cups whole milk
- approx. 2 ounces roux (made by blending 1 ounce/1¾ tablespoons softened butter with 1 ounce/3 tablespoons plain flour in a small bowl)
- ¼ teaspoon Dijon mustard
- 1½–2 cups grated Cheddar cheese or 1 cup grated Parmesan cheese
- 1 tablespoon chopped dill (optional)
- sea salt flakes and freshly ground black pepper

FOR THE PANGRATTATO
- 3½–5 tablespoons extra virgin olive oil
- 1 garlic clove, finely chopped
- 1 cup soft white breadcrumbs

Preheat the oven to 350°F.

To make the pangrattato, combine all the ingredients in a little bowl and set aside.

Skin the fish and cut it into 6 or 8 portions. Season with salt and pepper.

Place the bay leaves in a lightly buttered sauté pan or gratin dish and lay the pieces of fish on top. Cover with the milk and bring slowly to a boil. Simmer for 4–5 minutes or until the fish changes from translucent to opaque. Remove the fish with a slotted spoon to a plate and set aside.

Bring the milk back to a boil and whisk in the roux to thicken the sauce to a light coating consistency. Stir in the mustard and two-thirds of the grated cheese, and season to taste with salt and pepper. Add the dill, if using.

Return the fish to the pan and sprinkle the remaining cheese over the top, followed by the pangrattato.

Cook in the oven for 15–20 minutes or until the fish is heated through and the top is golden brown and crisp. Serve with a salad of organic leaves.

Bourride is far less well-known than the legendary French fish soup, bouillabaisse. Some versions puree the base of the soup, others add some tomato dice and mussels and occasionally potato. I love this version, but every Provençale *grandmère* and chef has their own.

Bourride *with saffron mayo*

- 3½ tablespoons extra virgin olive oil
- 6 ounces onion, chopped (about 1½ cups)
- 4 leeks, use white and pale green parts (save dark green leaves for stock), diced or cut into ⅛–¼-inch slices
- 12 ounces fennel, cut into ¾-inch dice
- 6 ounces carrots, peeled and cut into ¾-inch dice
- 18 ounces potatoes, sliced, or cut into 1-inch dice
- 1 bay leaf
- scant ⅔ cup dry white wine
- 3¾ cups homemade fish stock
- a good pinch of saffron threads, soaked in 2 tablespoons stock
- thinly sliced zest of 1 organic orange
- 4 pounds haddock or monkfish tail on the bone (or a mixture), cut into steaks 1½ inches thick, across the bone
- 9 ounces peeled shrimp (optional)
- sea salt flakes, freshly ground black pepper, and a good pinch of cayenne pepper
- chervil or flat-leaf parsley sprigs, to serve

FOR THE SAFFRON MAYO
- 2 organic, free-range egg yolks
- 1–4 garlic cloves, crushed with about ¼ teaspoon salt
- ¼ teaspoon Dijon mustard
- 2 teaspoons white wine vinegar
- scant 1 cup sunflower, peanut, or olive oil, or a mixture
- ½ teaspoon saffron threads, soaked in 2 teaspoons water
- 2 teaspoons chopped flat-leaf parsley (optional)

Heat the olive oil in a saucepan and add the onion, leek, fennel, carrots, potatoes, and bay leaf. Season well with salt and pepper. Cover and cook over gentle heat for 8–10 minutes, add the dry white wine, increase the heat, and continue to cook for 4–5 minutes or until the wine is reduced. Add the hot fish stock and saffron. Return to a boil, add the orange zest, fish, and shrimp, if raw. (Add later if cooked.)

Return to a boil and simmer very gently for 3–5 minutes until the fish is just cooked. Remove the orange peel and bay leaf. (The dish can be prepared ahead to this point.)

To make the saffron mayo, put the egg yolks into a bowl with the garlic salt, mustard, and vinegar (keep the egg whites to make meringues). Put the oil into a large measuring cup. Take a whisk in one hand and the oil in the other and drip the oil onto the egg yolks, drop by drop, whisking at the same time. Within a minute you will notice that the mixture is beginning to thicken. When this happens, you can add the oil a little faster, but don't get too cheeky or it will suddenly curdle because the egg yolks can only absorb the oil at a certain pace. Add the saffron and parsley. Stir to combine. Taste and add a little more seasoning and vinegar if necessary.

Whisk 3½ tablespoons of the broth into half the saffron mayo. Stir gently into the bourride. Season to taste and serve in wide soup bowls with chervil or parsley. Serve the remaining mayo and a toasted baguette or sourdough as accompaniments.

SERVES 2

A very simple "master recipe," which can be used not only for plaice, turbot, or brill but also for other flatfish, such as dabs, flounder, sole, and lemon sole. Depending on the size of the fish, you can serve this recipe as an appetizer or a main course. It's also delicious served with hollandaise sauce, mousseline, or beurre blanc in place of the herb butter.

Baked plaice, turbot, or brill
with potatoes, fennel & herb butter

- 1 pound potatoes, peeled and thinly sliced
- 6 ounces onions, thinly sliced
  (about 1¼ cups)
- ½ fennel bulb, very thinly sliced
- extra virgin olive oil, for drizzling
- 1 x 2¼–3¾-pound fresh plaice, turbot,
  brill, or other flat fish on the bone
- sea salt flakes and freshly ground
  black pepper

FOR THE HERB BUTTER
- ½ cup softened butter
- 4 teaspoons finely chopped mixed
  herbs, such as flat-leaf parsley,
  chives, fennel, and thyme leaves

Preheat the oven to 500°F.

Toss together the thinly sliced potatoes, onions, and fennel in a bowl. Drizzle lightly with extra virgin olive oil, season with salt, and spread evenly on an approx. 12 x 20-inch baking sheet. Bake for 5 minutes while you prepare the fish.

Turn the fish on its side and remove the head if you wish; I prefer to leave the fish whole. Wash the fish and clean the slit by the head very thoroughly. Using a sharp knife, cut through the skin right around the fish, just where the "fringe" meets the flesh. Be careful to cut neatly and to cross the side cuts at the tail or it will be difficult to remove the skin later on.

Season both sides of the fish with salt and pepper and lay on top of the partly cooked vegetables. Bake for 17–20 minutes until the vegetables are tender and the fish is cooked. To check if the fish is cooked, lift the flesh from the bone at the head: once it is ready, it should lift off the bone easily and be quite white with no traces of pink.

To make the herb butter, mix the softened butter in a little bowl with the herbs.

Just before you are about to serve, catch the skin down near the tail of the fish and pull it off gently (the skin will tear badly if it hasn't been properly cut). Lift the two fillets onto a hot plate and coat with the herb butter. Raise the tail and carefully lift the bone off the remainder of the fish. Break at the head and put aside. Carefully lift the remaining two fillets onto the plate. Coat with the herb butter and surround with the potatoes, onions, and fennel, which should be deliciously charred at the edges. Serve immediately.

Fishcakes are absolutely delicious when they are carefully made and served hot with a small dollop of herb or garlic butter melting on top. Try them here with scallion aioli. Don't be afraid to experiment—a little horseradish cream added to the fishcakes gives extra oomph! I have also experimented with a little grated ginger and chopped dill or lemongrass. For a spicy variation, follow the recipe below and add 1–2 seeded and chopped chilies with the onion. You could also substitute freshly chopped cilantro for the parsley if you wish. Accompany with a tomato and chili sauce and garnish with sprigs of fresh cilantro.

Fishcakes *with scallion aioli*

- 1¾ tablespoons butter
- 3¾ ounces onions, finely chopped
  (about 1 cup)
- 3¾ ounces mashed potato
- 1 pound 10 ounces cold leftover fish,
  such as salmon, cod, haddock, or hake
  (a proportion of smoked fish, such as
  smoked haddock or mackerel, is good)
- 1 organic, free-range egg yolk or small egg
- 1 tablespoon chopped flat-leaf parsley
- seasoned all-purpose flour, for dusting
- 1 beaten organic, free-range egg,
  for coating
- 2–2¾ ounces fresh white breadcrumbs
  or panko crumbs
- 1¾ tablespoons butter (preferably
  clarified, see page 16)
- 2 tablespoons extra virgin olive oil
- sea salt flakes and freshly ground
  black pepper

FOR THE SCALLION AIOLI
- ½ x quantity Aioli (page 96)
- 2 tablespoons finely chopped scallions
  (both white and green parts)

To make the fishcakes, melt the butter in a frying pan, stir in the onion, and sweat over gentle heat, covered, for 4–5 minutes until soft but not colored. Scrape the contents of the pan into a bowl and carefully stir in the mashed potato, flaked cooked fish, egg, and chopped parsley. Season to taste with salt and pepper. Form the mixture into fishcakes, approx. 2 ounces each or larger if you prefer. Coat each one first in the seasoned flour, then in the beaten egg, and finally in the breadcrumbs. Set aside on a plate and chill until needed.

To make the aioli, combine the aioli with the chopped scallions in a bowl.

Heat the butter and oil in the frying pan over low to medium heat and fry the fishcakes for about 3 minutes (depending on thickness) on each side until heated through and golden. Serve piping hot with a dollop of scallion aioli on top. A good green salad and some Tomato Fondue (page 133) make perfect accompaniments.

One of my favorite monkfish dishes. Hake, haddock,
or wild salmon also work here, but cut the fish into
individual portions rather than chunks. Serve with lots
of rice or pasta to mop up the delicious juices.

Monkfish poached
with tomatoes & Swiss chard

- 2¼ pounds monkfish, well-trimmed and
  cut into 4½-ounce pieces
- 12 ounces Swiss chard
- 4 tablespoons extra virgin olive oil
- 3¾ ounces onions, peeled and cut in half
  lengthwise, then cut crosswise into
  fine half rings
- 2-ounce piece of fresh ginger, peeled
  and cut into very fine slivers
- 1 x 14-ounce can of plum tomatoes,
  chopped, with their juice
- scant ½ cup thick coconut milk
- scant ⅔ cup water
- sea salt flakes, freshly ground black
  pepper, and a sprinkling of pul biber
  (Aleppo pepper)

Season both sides of the monkfish pieces with salt, pepper,
and a sprinkling of pul biber. Set aside for 15 minutes.

Remove the central stems from the Swiss chard and cut them
crosswise into strips ⅛ inch wide. Roll the green leaves and cut
crosswise into strips ¼ inch wide.

Heat the oil in a wide sauté pan over medium-high heat.
When it is hot, add the onions, ginger, and chard stems and
sauté for 5 minutes, stirring. Add the chopped tomatoes and
continue to cook for a further 5 minutes. Pour in the coconut
milk and water, and season with 1 teaspoon of salt and some
pepper. Bring to a boil, stirring, then simmer over low heat for
1 minute. The recipe can be prepared to this point ahead of
time and reheated.

To serve, bring the sauce to a simmer once again. Stir in the
chard leaves and simmer for a minute or two. Lay the fish in a
single layer over the top of the sauce and spoon some of the
sauce over the fish. Cover with a lid and simmer very gently for
8–10 minutes or until the fish is just cooked through. Season
to taste. Serve with pilaf rice or fresh pasta, if you wish, or just
some good bread to mop up the juices.

An inspired way to cook whole fillets of fish, I've given three separate sauce suggestions here but even a simple dill butter makes roast fish into a feast. Needless to say, other fish, such as haddock, hake, ling, cod, or pollock can be cooked in exactly the same way.

Roast fish *three ways*

- 1 whole wild fresh salmon
- melted butter or extra virgin olive oil, about 2 tablespoons of each
- sea salt flakes and freshly ground black pepper

FOR THE TOMATO & DILL TOPPING
- 4–8 tablespoons chopped dill
- 4–6 ripe tomatoes, seeded and diced, sprinkled with some sea salt flakes, freshly ground black pepper, and sugar
- scant ½–scant 1 cup extra virgin olive oil

Preheat the oven to 500°F.

Descale the salmon, fillet and remove the pin bones. For the topping, mix the dill and diced seasoned tomato together with the extra virgin olive oil.

Line a baking sheet with parchment paper. Put the fillets of fish on top. Brush with the melted butter or extra virgin olive oil. Season with salt and pepper. Spoon the dill and tomato oil over the surface. Roast for 8–10 minutes or until cooked and tender.

Serve in the pan or transfer the salmon onto one or two hot serving dishes. Sprinkle with a little fresh dill and dill flowers. Serve immediately with a salad of organic green leaves.

Variations
ROAST SALMON WITH TERIYAKI SAUCE
To make the teriyaki sauce, put 7 tablespoons of light or dark soy sauce, 7 tablespoons dry white wine, 2 large, thinly sliced garlic cloves, a 1½-inch piece of fresh ginger, peeled and thinly sliced, 2 tablespoons of wholegrain mustard, and 2 tablespoons of brown sugar into a stainless-steel saucepan. Bring to a boil and simmer for 3–4 minutes. (Alternatively, spoon over the fish before putting it in the oven.) Roast the fish as above. Brush the fish generously with the teriyaki sauce, sprinkle with fresh cilantro, and serve.

ROAST SALMON WITH PUL BIBER
Prepare the salmon as above, drizzle with extra virgin olive oil. Sprinkle with pul biber (Aleppo pepper) and sea salt flakes. Roast as above. Serve with a good green salad.

SERVES 8-10

This is a tradition in San Francisco, but I first enjoyed it at my friend Mary Risley's table, who ran Tante Marie's Cooking School. She kindly shared the recipe for this substantial meal in a pot—you'll love it. All you need is some bread for dunking.

Californian cioppino

- 24 well-scrubbed live clams or cockles
- 2 onions, chopped
- 2 tablespoons extra virgin olive oil,
  plus extra to drizzle
- 3 garlic cloves, chopped
- 1 fennel bulb, chopped
- 2½ pounds fresh tomatoes, peeled
  (see page 112), seeded, and chopped
  or 3 x 14-ounce cans of Italian plum
  tomatoes
- 1 tablespoon tomato paste (optional)
- 2 cups dry white wine
- ½ teaspoon red pepper flakes
- 1¾ tablespoons chopped oregano
  or sweet marjoram
- 2 pounds fresh white fish, such as
  sea bass, rock cod, halibut, or monkfish
- 1 pound scallops (optional)
- 1 pound raw shrimp
- brown and white meat from 1 large
  cooked crab (optional)
- 1 ounce flat-leaf parsley, chopped
- sea salt flakes and freshly ground
  black pepper
- sourdough bread, to serve

First steam the clams or cockles. Place them in a heavy-based pot with 1 inch of water. Cover and cook over high heat, shaking occasionally, until the shells open. Set aside in a bowl, reserving the broth, and keep covered until ready to use.

To make the soup base, put the onions into the pot with ½ teaspoon of salt and a generous splash of olive oil. Cook, stirring from time to time, until the onions are soft. Stir in the garlic and cook for another minute or two. Add the fennel, tomatoes, tomato paste, wine, red pepper flakes, and oregano.

Carefully strain the broth from the steamed clams into the pot, leaving behind the last tablespoon or so as it will probably be very gritty. Bring to a boil, stirring, and simmer gently for 20 minutes.

Meanwhile, cut the white fish into large chunks, drizzle lightly with olive oil, and season with salt and pepper.

Remove the muscle from each scallop and peel the shrimp. Place the shellfish on a clean plate, drizzle lightly with olive oil, and season with salt and pepper.

About 15 minutes before you are ready to serve, bring the soup base to a boil, stirring. Carefully fold in the chunks of white fish, cover with a lid, and simmer for 5 minutes.

Carefully fold in the scallops and shrimp and simmer gently for a further 5 minutes. Stir in the steamed clams and crab meat, if using. Season to taste. Then cover the pan with a lid and set aside for a minute or two.

Sprinkle with lots of parsley and serve in warmed bowls with sourdough bread to mop up all the juices.

Who doesn't love a fish pie? This super-easy recipe can be used for almost any round fish, including cod, pollock, ling. haddock, salmon, or gray mullet. I like to prepare a big batch to make several pies, which can be refrigerated or frozen and reheated another day. A chopped hard-boiled egg and a cup of cooked peas add extra nourishment and flavor. Here I use a scrunchy phyllo topping, but I often make a crispy Cheddar crumb or mashed potato topping.

Mermaid's fish pie

- 2½ pounds cod, hake, haddock, or gray mullet fillets, or a mixture
- 1 tablespoon butter, for greasing
- 2½ cups cold whole milk
- approx. ¾ ounce roux (made by blending 2 teaspoons softened butter with 3½ teaspoons all-purpose flour)
- ¼ teaspoon Dijon mustard
- 1½–1¾ cups grated Gruyère or Cheddar cheese or 1 cup grated Parmesan cheese
- 2 tablespoons chopped flat-leaf parsley
- 3¾ ounces shelled cooked mussels
- 3¾ ounces peeled cooked shrimp
- ½ can of chopped anchovies, approx. 4 fillets (optional)
- 4 sheets of phyllo pastry
- melted butter, for brushing
- sea salt flakes and freshly ground black pepper

Variations

MERMAID'S FISH PIE WITH SEAWEED BUTTER

Cream ½ cup softened butter with 2 tablespoons of finely chopped dulse seaweed and a few drops of lemon juice in a small bowl. Form into a roll. Wrap the roll in wax paper or foil, twisting each end to seal, and refrigerate to harden. Cut into 6–8 portions and serve with the fish pie.

Preheat the oven to 350°F.

Skin the fish and cut into 6–8 portions. Season well with salt and pepper. Lay the pieces of fish in a lightly buttered 10½-inch sauté pan and cover with the cold milk. Bring to a boil, then simmer for 4–5 minutes until the fish has changed from translucent to opaque. Remove the fish to a plate with a slotted spoon.

Bring the milk back to a boil and whisk in enough of the roux to thicken the sauce to a light coating consistency. Stir in the mustard, grated cheese, and chopped parsley. Season to taste with salt and pepper. Add the cooked fish together with the mussels, shrimp, and chopped anchovies, and stir gently to coat with the sauce.

Brush each phyllo sheet with melted butter and cut into four pieces. Scrunch up each piece of phyllo pastry and arrange side by side on top of the pie.

Bake in the oven for 15–20 minutes until the pie is bubbling and the phyllo is crisp and crunchy.

Hake, cod, or monkfish also work deliciously with
this sweet pepper stew. Add 1½ cups diced cooked
potato to the base for an extra-filling supper.

Spanish red pepper stew *with haddock*

- 2 tablespoons extra virgin olive oil,
  plus extra to serve
- 1 garlic clove, crushed
- 8 ounces onions, sliced (about 1½ cups)
- 2½ tablespoons dry sherry
- 4 red bell peppers
- 1 red or green chili, sliced
- 6 large tomatoes (dark red and very ripe)
- a pinch of saffron threads
- a few fresh basil leaves
- 4 x 6-ounce haddock fillets
- 1–2 teaspoons smoked paprika
- sea salt flakes, freshly ground black
  pepper, and sugar
- plenty of chopped flat-leaf parsley,
  to serve

Heat 2 tablespoons of olive oil over gentle heat in a 10-inch/
3-quart casserole, add the garlic, and cook for a few seconds.
Add the sliced onions, toss in the oil, and soften over gentle
heat for 5–6 minutes. Pour in the sherry, bring to a boil, and
reduce for 5–6 minutes.

Halve the bell peppers, removing the seeds and stalks. Cut the
peppers into quarters and then into ¾–1-inch squares. Add to
the pan with the chili and stir to combine. Cover with a lid and
cook for 5–6 minutes while you prepare the tomatoes.

Scald the tomatoes in boiling water for 10 seconds, then pour
off the water and slip off the skins. Slice the tomatoes and
add to the stew with the saffron. Season with salt, pepper, and
sugar, and throw in the basil. Cook for 20 minutes, covered,
until the vegetables are just soft.

Season the fish fillets with salt, pepper, and some smoked
paprika. Lay the fish on top of the softened vegetables, cover
with a lid, and cook for 4–5 minutes until the fish changes from
translucent to opaque. Sprinkle a little more smoked paprika
over the top of each piece of fish.

Serve as soon as possible, scattered with parsley and drizzled
with extra virgin olive oil. Accompany with lots of crusty
sourdough and a good salad of organic leaves.

VEGETABLES

This recipe is based on a thick unctuous soup that Naomi Duguid and her friends cooked for lunch at the UK's Oxford Food Symposium 2018. I'm crazy about purslane and try to encourage everyone I meet to grow it. Once established, it spreads rapidly so be careful where you plant it. I use it in a million different ways—in soups, salads, stews... It's very nutritious and grows wild in many areas. I've heard that it's classed as a noxious weed in the US—it even grows up through cracks in the pavement—but my answer would just be to eat it. Few foods are so full of good things as this juicy little succulent.

Purslane soup

- scant 1¼ cups French lentils, rinsed and picked over
- 2 ounces onions, finely chopped (about ½ cup)
- ½ cup arborio or other short-grain rice, washed and drained
- 7¾ cups vegetable stock or water
- 3 tablespoons tomato paste
- 1 teaspoon ground cumin
- ½ teaspoon ground turmeric
- 3 teaspoons sea salt, to taste (you may need more)
- 9¾ ounces purslane leaves and stems, finely chopped
- coarsely cracked black pepper
- extra virgin olive oil, to drizzle

TO SERVE
- 8 warm flatbreads
- 4½ ounces hard goat or sheep cheese, crumbled (about 1 cup)
- 8 organic lemon wedges
- a generous quantity of fresh herbs: I use little sprigs of flat-leaf parsley, tarragon, chervil, mint, and lovage
- a few scallions, sliced on the diagonal

Put the lentils, onions, and rice into a 10-inch/3-quart saucepan and cover with the stock (or water, as a last resort). Bring to a rolling boil, stirring all the time. Skim off any foam that forms on the surface, then cover and reduce the heat to a gentle simmer. Cook for 20 minutes, covered, until the lentils are tender—you might need to add a little more stock or water, if necessary.

Stir in the tomato paste, cumin, turmeric, and 2 teaspoons of salt, then add the purslane and stir thoroughly. Cook for about 20 minutes or until the purslane is very soft and the flavors have blended. Season to taste. The soup should be thick and unctuous, but if you prefer a thinner soup you could add a further 1¼ cups of stock.

Ladle into individual bowls, sprinkle with coarsely cracked black pepper, and drizzle with extra virgin olive oil. Bring the flatbreads, cheese, lemon wedges, sprigs of fresh herbs, and scallions to the table and let everyone add their own toppings.

This is a gorgeous eggplant dish. The spiced eggplant mixture is also good served cold or at room temperature as an accompaniment to hot or cold lamb or pork. We grow several varieties of eggplant at Ballymaloe, but look out for Slim Jim for this dish—it's one of my favorites. You can add $3\frac{1}{4}$ cups of diced cooked potatoes instead of the chickpeas, if you wish, but you'll also need to add $\frac{2}{3}$ cup of vegetable or chicken stock to keep the sauce nice and juicy.

Spiced eggplant *with goat cheese, chickpeas & arugula*

- 1-inch piece of fresh ginger, peeled and coarsely chopped
- 6 large garlic cloves, coarsely crushed
- 3½ tablespoons water
- approx. 1 cup extra virgin olive oil
- 1¾ pounds eggplants, cut into slices ¾ inch thick
- 1 teaspoon whole fennel seeds
- 2 teaspoons whole cumin seeds
- 12 ounces very ripe tomatoes, peeled and finely chopped or 1 x 14-ounce can of chopped tomatoes, plus 1 teaspoon sugar
- 1 tablespoon ground coriander
- ¼ teaspoon ground turmeric
- ½ teaspoon cayenne pepper
- ⅓ cup raisins
- 1 x 14-ounce can of chickpeas, drained and rinsed
- 3¾ ounces soft goat cheese
- fresh arugula leaves
- sea salt flakes
- lots of crusty bread, to serve (optional)

Put the ginger, garlic, and water into a blender and blend until fairly smooth.

Heat ¾ cup of the oil in a 10–12-inch sauté pan. When it is hot and almost smoking, add a few of the eggplant slices and cook until tender and golden on both sides. Remove and drain on a wire rack over a baking sheet. Repeat with the remaining eggplant, adding more oil if necessary.

Heat 3 tablespoons of the oil in the pan. When hot, add the fennel and cumin seeds—careful not to let them burn—and stir just for a few seconds. Put in the chopped tomatoes, the ginger-garlic mixture, the ground coriander and turmeric, a pinch of cayenne, and some salt. Simmer for 5–6 minutes, stirring occasionally, until the mixture thickens slightly.

Add the fried eggplant slices, raisins, and chickpeas, and stir gently to coat them in the spicy sauce. Cover the pan with a lid, reduce the heat to very low, and cook for 3–4 minutes. The dish can be prepared ahead to this point.

To serve, drop dollops of the soft goat cheese over the surface, scatter with some fresh arugula leaves, and drizzle with a little extra virgin olive oil. Serve warm with lots of crusty bread, if you wish.

This gorgeous tart was inspired by a photo on the cover of a magazine. The ricotta and pecorino filling is uncooked, so be sure to assemble the tart close to the time of eating. Best made in late summer or early fall when the tomatoes are exquisitely sweet. I use the delicious buffalo ricotta made in West Cork for this dish.

Heirloom tomato & ricotta tart

FOR THE PASTRY

- 1 cup plus 2 tablespoons all-purpose flour
- ⅓ cup cold butter
- a little water, to bind
- 1 beaten organic, free-range egg, to seal

FOR THE FILLING

- 9 ounces buffalo ricotta
- 3½ ounces pecorino cheese, grated (about 1⅓ cups)
- 2 tablespoons heavy cream
- 1 tablespoon extra virgin olive oil
- 1 tablespoon honey
- 2 tablespoons chopped basil, thyme, and marjoram, plus extra leaves to garnish
- zest of ½ organic lemon
- sea salt flakes
- ¼ teaspoon freshly cracked black pepper
- 1½ pounds mixed heritage and cherry tomatoes, including green zebra and red and yellow cherry tomatoes, if available

First make the pastry. All the ingredients should be cold. Sift the flour into a large bowl. Cut the butter into cubes. Toss the cubes into the flour and then proceed to lift up a few cubes of butter at the time in each hand. Using your thumbs, rub the cubes of butter across the middle three fingers, toward the index fingers.

Allow the flakes of floured butter to drop back into the bowl, then pick up some more and continue until all the butter is rubbed in. As you rub in the butter, hold your hands well above the bowl and run your fingers through the flour to incorporate as much air as possible to keep the mixture cool. This whole process should only take a minute or two—careful not to rub the butter in too much, or the pastry will be heavy. The pieces should resemble lumpy breadcrumbs. If you are in doubt, shake the bowl and any larger pieces will come to the top. Add salt if using unsalted butter.

Using a fork, toss and stir the pastry as you add just enough water to bind—2–3 tablespoons should do the trick. If you are in doubt, discard the fork and collect up the pastry with your hand; you will be able to judge more easily by feel if it needs a little more water. Be careful not to make the pastry too wet or it will shrink in the oven. If the pastry is too dry, it will be difficult to roll out.

When the pastry has come together, turn it out onto the work surface and flatten it into an approx. 12-inch round. Cover with wax paper or plastic wrap and, if possible, set aside in the refrigerator to rest for at least 15 minutes to allow the gluten to relax. The pastry will then be less likely to shrink in the oven.

Preheat the oven to 350°F.

Roll out the pastry to a circle approx. 10-inch in diameter. Lift the pastry over a 9-inch greased tart pan and press down gently around the sides. Trim around the edges with a sharp knife and prick the base gently with a fork. Line with parchment paper and fill with baking beans.

Transfer the pastry shell to the oven and bake "blind" for about 25 minutes until pale and golden. Remove the baking beans and paper. Brush the part-baked pastry shell all over with a little beaten egg and pop it back into the oven for 5–10 minutes until pale golden brown all over. Set aside to cool.

To make the filling, combine the ricotta and pecorino in a bowl. Add the heavy cream, extra virgin olive oil, honey, herbs, lemon zest, salt, and pepper. Mix gently together. Taste a little dollop of the filling with a slice of tomato and correct the seasoning, if necessary. It might need a little more honey.

Slice the larger tomatoes and cut the smaller cherry ones in half lengthwise or crosswise, as you prefer.

Not long before serving, spoon the ricotta filling into the cooked pastry shell and arrange the tomatoes on top. I like to arrange the sliced, bigger ones, including the green zebra over the base and top with the smaller cherry tomatoes. Season with salt, pepper, a little drizzle of honey (about ½ teaspoon), and lots of thyme and marjoram leaves. Garnish with a few little basil leaves and serve soon.

One of the very best vegetarian one-pot dishes. What's not to like about black-eyed peas, chickpeas, and pumpkin with lots of spices? Delicious on its own, but equally good with a roast chicken or a few lamb chops. Eat with flatbreads or pilaf rice, if you prefer.

Black-eyed pea, pumpkin & chickpea stew

- 6 tablespoons extra virgin olive oil
- 1 teaspoon cumin seeds
- 1 x 1-inch cinnamon stick
- 5½ ounces onions, chopped (about 1⅓ cups)
- 4 garlic cloves, very finely chopped
- 8 ounces fresh mushrooms, sliced approx. ⅛-inch thick (about 4 cups)
- 1 pound pumpkin or butternut squash, peeled and cut in ¾-inch cubes
- 14 ounces fresh tomatoes, peeled and chopped or 1 x 14-ounce can of chopped tomatoes
- 2 teaspoons ground coriander
- 1 teaspoon ground cumin
- ½ teaspoon ground turmeric
- a pinch of sugar
- ¼ teaspoon cayenne pepper
- 1 pound (about 3 cups) cooked black-eyed peas, strained (reserving the cooking liquid)
- 8 ounces (about 1⅔ cups) cooked chickpeas, strained (reserving the cooking liquid)
- 1 teaspoon salt
- freshly ground black pepper
- 3 tablespoons chopped cilantro

FOR THE MINT YOGURT
- 1⅓ cups plain yogurt
- 1 tablespoon chopped mint leaves

Heat the oil in a sauté pan over medium-high heat. When it is hot, put in the cumin seeds and the cinnamon stick. Let them sizzle for 5–6 seconds, then add the onions and garlic. Stir-fry for 3–4 minutes until the onion is just beginning to color at the edges. Add the mushrooms and cook until the mushrooms wilt, then add the pumpkin or squash, tomatoes, ground coriander, cumin and turmeric, a pinch of sugar, and the cayenne. Cook for 1 minute, stirring, then cover with a lid and cook over gentle heat for 10 minutes.

Turn off the heat and tip in the drained beans and chickpeas. Add the salt and pepper, together with 2 tablespoons of the cilantro. Pour in scant ⅔ cup of the bean cooking liquid and ⅔ cup of the chickpea liquid (or 1¼ cups of vegetable stock if you've used canned pulses). Return to a boil, and then reduce the heat and simmer for 10–15 minutes, stirring occasionally, until the beans and chickpeas are tender.

To make the mint yogurt, combine the yogurt with the chopped mint in a bowl.

Remove the cinnamon stick from the pan before serving and sprinkle with the remaining cilantro. Spoon into serving bowls and top with a dollop of the mint yogurt. Accompany with a good green salad and rice, if you wish.

A delicious, fresh-tasting vegetarian appetizer or small plate, bursting with clean fresh flavors. Best eaten immediately, otherwise the vegetable mixture becomes very watery.

Cauliflower ceviche on corn tostado *with chili mayo & avocado*

- 8 x 4-inch crisp corn tostados
- 2 ripe avocados, peeled and cut into chunky slices crosswise
- fresh herb sprigs, such as cilantro, sweet cicely, or flat-leaf parsley, to serve

FOR THE CHILI MAYONNAISE
- 1½ tablespoons pureed chipotle chilies in adobo
- juice of 1 lime (optional)
- 1 tablespoon chopped cilantro
- 1 cup homemade mayonnaise
- a pinch of salt

FOR THE "CEVICHE"
- 4 tablespoons finely diced cauliflower (approx. ¼-inch cubes)
- 4 tablespoons finely diced cucumber (unpeeled)
- 4 tablespoons finely diced tomato (seeds discarded)
- 2 tablespoons finely diced onion
- 1 teaspoon chopped red chili, or to taste
- 2 tablespoons roughly chopped cilantro
- juice of 1 organic lime
- sea salt flakes and freshly ground black pepper

For the chili mayo, stir the pureed chipotle chilies, lime juice, and fresh cilantro into the mayonnaise and add a pinch of salt.

Mix all the ingredients for the ceviche together in a bowl.

To serve, spread some of the chili mayo on each tostado, top with a couple of spoonfuls of the cauliflower ceviche, and finish with a few slices of avocado and some herbs.

Enjoy immediately.

At Ballymaloe we make gorgeous, thick, unctuous yogurt from the milk of our small Jersey herd. I love to serve herb-flavored yogurt with lots of dishes, such as this one, as well as plain rice.

Zucchini *with yogurt & fresh herbs*

- 4 zucchini, 4½–6 inches long
- 4 tablespoons extra virgin olive oil
- generous ½ cup thick plain yogurt
- 1 fat garlic clove, crushed or finely grated
- 1 teaspoon honey
- lots of freshly snipped herbs, such as dill, chervil, and tarragon
- sea salt flakes and freshly ground black pepper
- borage or hyssop flowers (optional), to garnish
- sourdough bread, to serve

Heat a heavy-based griddle pan over high heat. Slice the zucchini lengthwise into ¼-inch strips. Drizzle with extra virgin olive oil and season with salt and pepper.

Cook a few at a time in the hot pan until soft and marked by the griddle on both sides. Transfer to a platter and arrange side by side.

Mix the yogurt with the garlic and honey in a small bowl, and season with a little salt.

Drizzle the yogurt mixture generously over the zucchini and scatter with plenty of herb sprigs. Pretty blue borage or hyssop flowers look lovely sprinkled over the top, if available, as, of course, do zucchini blossoms.

Serve with crusty sourdough bread.

Roast cauliflower is a brilliant vehicle for myriad flavors. For minimum effort, just scatter the roasted cauliflower with chopped parsley or a generous dusting of freshly grated Parmesan or frozen blue cheese, which is so easy to grate.

Roast cauliflower *with anchovies, peppers & herbs*

- 1 medium cauliflower, weighing approx. 3 pounds 2 ounces
- ⅓–½ cup butter
- 2 teaspoons thyme leaves or 1 teaspoon finely chopped rosemary
- salt

FOR THE TOPPING
- 1 tablespoon chopped flat-leaf parsley
- 1 garlic clove, crushed
- 2 ounces piquillo pepper or ripe cherry tomatoes, chopped
- 1½ tablespoons chopped anchovies
- 4–6 tablespoons extra virgin olive oil
- 1 teaspoon finely grated organic lemon zest
- ¼ cup toasted sliced almonds

Variation
SPICY CAULIFLOWER
Cook the cauliflower as above. Instead of making the thyme butter, heat 6 tablespoons of extra virgin olive oil, 2 teaspoons of ground cumin, 2 teaspoons of ground coriander, 1 teaspoon of ground turmeric, and 1 teaspoon of pul biber (Aleppo pepper) in the casserole and cook for 1 minute. Add the cauliflower and baste in the spicy oil before cooking in the oven for 5–6 minutes, uncovered. Sprinkle with sea salt and 2 teaspoons of chopped cilantro before serving.

Preheat the oven to 450°F.

First prepare the cauliflower. Remove the outer leaves from the cauliflower and trim the base. Cut a deep cross in the base, then remove the rest of the leaves and cut the stalk into 1½-inch pieces. Pour ¾ inch of water into an 8½-inch ovenproof casserole, approx. 4 inches deep, season with plenty of salt, and bring to a boil. Put the chopped leaves and stalk into the bottom of the pan and place the cauliflower head on top. Cover the pan with a lid and simmer for 4 minutes, then remove the lid and cook for a further 2 minutes. Remove the cauliflower and leaves to a plate and tip out any water in the pan.

Melt the butter in the casserole and allow it to become golden brown—be careful it doesn't burn. Quickly add the thyme leaves, then the cooked cauliflower. Baste the cauliflower with the thyme butter and then transfer the pan to the hot oven to cook for 15–20 minutes, uncovered. Regular basting, though not essential, makes it even more delicious. To test for doneness, pierce the base with a skewer.

Meanwhile, mix all of the ingredients for the topping together in a bowl, apart from the sliced almonds. Spoon the topping over the roasted cauliflower and sprinkle with the toasted, sliced almonds. Serve with crusty bread, if you wish.

Spanakopita can also be made in individual "snails," but this delicious flaky version comes in a sauté pan. This version is good for a feast as it serves 12–15 people. You can halve the recipe if you're serving smaller numbers.

Spanakopita Greek spinach & cheese pie

- ⅔ cup butter
- 2 pounds leeks, sliced and washed really well
- 6 tablespoons extra virgin olive oil
- 18 ounces onions, finely chopped (about 4 cups)
- 8 scallions (both white and green parts), finely sliced
- 2 pounds fresh spinach, weighed after the stalks have been removed, washed really well
- 6 tablespoons chopped flat-leaf parsley
- 6 tablespoons chopped dill
- 12 ounces feta cheese, crumbled (about 3 cups)
- 4½ ounces Parmesan cheese, grated (about 1½ cups)
- 4 organic, free-range eggs, beaten
- 9 sheets of phyllo pastry, 12 x 17 inches
- 1 tablespoon melted butter, for brushing
- egg wash, made by beating 1 organic, free-range egg with 2–3 tablespoons whole milk
- sea salt flakes, freshly ground black pepper, and nutmeg

Preheat the oven to 350°F.

Melt the butter in a 10½-inch ovenproof sauté pan and cook the sliced leeks with 2–3 tablespoons of water for 4–5 minutes until tender (older leeks may take slightly longer). Scoop the leeks out of the pan and set aside on a plate while you cook the spinach.

Heat the olive oil in the sauté pan, add the onions and scallions, and sweat over low heat for 3–4 minutes, covered, until soft but not colored. Increase the heat to medium, add the spinach and toss well to coat it in the oil. Season with salt, pepper, and nutmeg. Add the chopped parsley and dill, and continue to cook for 4–5 minutes, stirring, until the spinach has wilted. Turn out the spinach mixture into a colander and set aside to drain and cool.

Combine the crumbled feta and 1¼ cups of the grated Parmesan in a medium bowl and beat in the egg. Add the well-drained spinach and the leeks and season to taste.

Brushing each sheet of phyllo with melted butter as you go, layer up the pastry in the base of the sauté pan or a baking dish so that it comes up the sides, leaving enough pastry hanging over the sides to fold over and encase the filling.

Spread the filling evenly over the pastry and bring up the sides of the phyllo to enclose the filling. Score the top of the pie in a diamond or square pattern and brush all over with the egg wash. Sprinkle the surface with the remaining grated Parmesan.

Bake for about 45 minutes until puffed up and golden.

Serve, cut into wedges, while still warm and fluffy.

Cheddar cheese fondue sounds so retro, but it's a brilliant one-pot supper. Choose your seat carefully, because if you drop the bread into the fondue you must kiss the person on your right—this could be your big chance! My mother-in-law, Myrtle Allen, devised this cheese fondue recipe made from Irish Cheddar cheese. It's a huge favorite at Ballymaloe, as even though it's a meal in itself it can be made in minutes and is loved by adults and children alike. A fondue set is obviously an advantage, but not totally essential. Florets of cauliflower, Romanesco, or broccoli make good crunchy dippers.

Ballymaloe Cheddar cheese fondue

- 4 tablespoons dry white wine
- 4 small garlic cloves, crushed
- 4 teaspoons good tomato chutney
  (I use Ballymaloe Relish)
- 4 teaspoons chopped flat-leaf parsley
- scant 2 cups grated aged Cheddar cheese
- lots of crusty white bread, at least
  4 thick slices
- florets of cauliflower, Romanesco, or
  broccoli, or a mixture

Put the white wine, garlic, chutney, parsley, and cheese into a fondue pot or a small saucepan and stir to combine, off the heat.

Just before you are about to serve the fondue, put the fondue pot or small, heavy-based saucepan over low heat and cook until the cheese melts and begins to bubble—but don't stir. Transfer the pot to the fondue stove, if available, or use a heatproof stand, trivet, or mat and serve immediately.

Provide each guest with some fresh slices of bread, or cubes of bread crisped up slightly in a hot oven and a selection of chopped vegetables. They will also need a fondue fork and an ordinary fork.

This is one of my "go-to" recipes to feed a group of hungry friends. You can replace the chicken with leftover cooked pheasant, fish, or shellfish, if you like—monkfish works particularly well. Just think of the tomato fondue as a base for many good things.

Spicy tomato fondue
with many good things

FOR THE SPICY TOMATO FONDUE
- 2 tablespoons extra virgin olive oil
- 3¾ ounces onions, sliced (about ¾ cup)
- 1–2 chilies, seeded and finely chopped
- 2 teaspoons ground cumin
- 1 garlic clove, crushed
- 2 pounds very ripe tomatoes in summer, peeled (see page 112), or 2 x 14-ounce cans of chopped tomatoes in winter
- sea salt flakes, freshly ground black, pepper and sugar, to taste

FOR THE "MANY GOOD THINGS"
- 1½–2 pounds cooked chicken, cut into approx. 1-inch dice
- 6 cooked potatoes, cut into approx. ¾-inch dice
- lots of coarsely chopped flat-leaf parsley or cilantro

First make the tomato fondue. Heat the oil in a large stainless-steel sauté pan or casserole over gentle heat. Add the sliced onions, chopped chilies, ground cumin, and garlic, and stir well to coat everything in the oil. Cover the pan with a lid and sweat over gentle heat for about 10 minutes until the onions are soft, but not colored. It is vital that the onions are completely soft before you add the tomatoes.

Slice the peeled fresh tomatoes and add to the pan with their juices (if you are using canned tomatoes, you can tip them straight in). Season with salt, pepper, and sugar; canned tomatoes need lots of sugar because of their high acidity. Cover and cook for a further 10–20 minutes until the tomato softens, uncovering for the last 5 minutes or so to reduce the sauce a little. Fresh tomatoes need a shorter cooking time than canned ones to preserve their lively fresh flavor. Depending on how you plan to use your fondue, you might want to reduce it a bit further.

Add the cooked chicken and potatoes, bring to a boil and bubble away for 4–5 minutes. Season to taste and scatter with parsley or cilantro.

Serve with a salad of organic green leaves.

Everyone loves this North Indian vegetarian dish. If you're not too rushed, sauté the cubed paneer in a little oil beforehand until they are lightly colored, then pop them into a bowl of hot water until you are ready to add them to the sauce. Soaking the fried paneer in water really plumps it up, but make sure you drain it really well before adding it to the sauce. Feta cheese makes a good substitute if you can't get hold of paneer.

Matar paneer curry

- ½ tablespoon finely grated fresh ginger
- 2 teaspoons crushed garlic
- 3 tablespoons vegetable oil
- 1 teaspoon cumin seeds
- 3½ ounces onions, finely chopped (about ¾ cup)
- 4 ripe tomatoes, finely chopped into ⅛-inch dice
- 1 teaspoon chili powder
- 1 tablespoon ground coriander
- ½ teaspoon ground turmeric
- ½ teaspoon ground fenugreek
- ¾ teaspoon garam masala
- ¾ cup thick plain yogurt or labneh
- 9 ounces paneer or feta cheese, cut into 1-inch cubes
- 1½ cups fresh or frozen peas
- freshly squeezed organic lime juice, to taste
- salt, to taste
- chopped cilantro leaves, to serve

FOR THE CUCUMBER & YOGURT RAITA
- ¼ medium cucumber
- ½ tablespoon finely chopped onion
- ½ teaspoon cumin seeds
- ¾ cup plain yogurt
- 1 ripe tomato, finely diced (seeds discarded)
- 1 tablespoon chopped cilantro leaves
- sea salt flakes and freshly ground black pepper

First make the cucumber and yogurt raita. Peel the cucumber if you wish, cut it in half lengthwise and remove the seeds, then cut into ¼-inch dice. Put the diced cucumber into a bowl with the onion, sprinkle with salt, and set aside for 5–10 minutes.

Meanwhile, roast the cumin seeds in a pan to release their aroma, then crush lightly in a pestle and mortar.

Drain the cucumber, discarding the juices. Stir in the yogurt and add the tomato, cilantro, and cumin. Season to taste. Cover and chill until needed.

To make the curry, make a paste by combining the grated ginger with the crushed garlic in a little bowl.

Heat the oil in the saucepan and add the cumin seeds. Stir for a few seconds to release their aroma into the oil, then add the finely chopped onions and 1 teaspoon of the ginger and garlic paste. Stir over medium heat for 1–2 minutes until the onion begins to soften. Add the tomatoes, salt, and spices, and stir well to combine. Cover the pan with a lid and cook over gentle heat for 7–8 minutes until the tomatoes are soft and pulpy.

Whisk the plain yogurt or labneh in a medium bowl and add 6 tablespoons of the hot onion and tomato mixture, one tablespoon at a time, whisking well between each addition. Transfer the yogurt mixture back to the pan; return the pan to the heat and add the paneer (or feta) and peas. Simmer for 5 minutes, then remove the pan from the heat. Squeeze over some lime juice and taste, adding a little more if necessary. Scatter with cilantro and serve with the raita and some flatbreads or rice.

SERVES 6

There are various interpretations of the Kenyan name here, including "stretch the week" and "feed the week"—but either way, it's delicious. You can also cook a few lamb chops or chicken thighs or drumsticks while the sakuma is simmering, and pop them on top. Scatter with lots of oregano or chopped marjoram.

Sakuma wike
tomato & kale stew

- 2 teaspoons extra virgin olive oil
- 3¾ ounces onions, sliced (about ¾ cup)
- 1 garlic clove, crushed
- 1 sliced red chili (optional)
- 2 pounds very ripe tomatoes
  or 18 ounces fresh tomatoes
  and 1 x 14-ounce can of whole
  plum tomatoes
- 1 tablespoon chopped fresh herbs,
  such as thyme, flat-leaf parsley,
  mint, basil, lemon balm, or marjoram
  (or a mixture)
- generous 1 cup homemade vegetable
  stock or water
- 9 ounces kale, weighed after the stalks
  have been removed
- 3¾ ounces (about ¾ cup) cooked
  chickpeas (optional)
- sea salt flakes, freshly ground black
  pepper, and sugar, to taste
- chopped oregano or marjoram, to serve
  (optional)

Heat the olive oil in an 8½-inch/3½-quart casserole over gentle heat and sweat the onions, garlic, and chili, if using, for 5-6 minutes until soft. Cover the pan. It is vital for the success of this dish that the onions are completely soft before you add the tomatoes.

Remove the hard core from the fresh tomatoes. Put them into a deep bowl and cover with boiling water. Count to 10, then pour off the water and peel off the skins. Cut into slices, reserving the juice.

Add the fresh tomatoes (or canned tomatoes) to the pan and season with salt, pepper, and sugar. Add a generous sprinkling of chopped herbs and cook for 10–20 minutes or until the tomato softens.

Pour in scant ½ cup vegetable stock (or water) and bring to a boil. Add the roughly chopped kale and chickpeas, if using. Return to a boil, then cook for 8–10 minutes until the kale is tender. Season to taste and sprinkle with chopped oregano or marjoram, if you wish. Serve as is, or as an accompaniment to either grilled fish or meat dishes.

Fresh jackfruit is wonderful to use here but if it's not easy to find, use a can instead. Jackfruit has the texture of pulled pork so is a great vegan alternative to meat.

Jackfruit curry

- 2 tablespoons extra virgin olive oil
- 1 teaspoon mustard seeds
- 1 teaspoon cumin seeds
- 6 ounces onion, diced (about 1½ cups)
- 2 large garlic cloves, crushed
- 1 teaspoon freshly grated turmeric
- ½–1 teaspoon freshly grated ginger
- 1 teaspoon ground cumin
- 1 teaspoon ground coriander
- ¼ teaspoon chili flakes
- 1 pound peeled and chopped ripe tomatoes or 1 x 14-ounce can chopped tomatoes
- 1 x 14-ounce can chickpeas, drained
- 1 x 20-ounce can jackfruit, washed and drained (about 10½ ounces drained fruit)
- 4 tablespoons homemade vegetable stock or water
- sea salt flakes, freshly ground pepper, and sugar
- lots of fresh cilantro
- thick plain yogurt and organic lime wedges, to serve

Heat the oil in a sauté pan over medium heat, add the mustard seeds, then as soon as they splutter, add the cumin seeds and onion, and stir-fry for 4–5 minutes or until the onion starts to soften and caramelize a little. Add the garlic, turmeric, ginger, ground cumin and coriander, and chili flakes. Continue to stir-fry for 1–2 minutes. Add the peeled and chopped tomatoes, chickpeas, and jackfruit, and season with salt and pepper. Bring to a boil and simmer for 10–12 minutes (you may need to add a little water if it seems a bit dry). Season with salt, pepper, and sugar. Pour into a warm serving bowl and scatter with lots of fresh cilantro sprigs.

Provide a wedge of lime for each guest and offer thick plain yogurt as an accompaniment. Serve with rice or flatbreads, if you wish.

Bread and butter pudding can be savory as well as deliciously sweet. This version makes a tasty economical supper for six or more hungry people. There are myriad variations here—chorizo instead of bacon; scallions or melted leeks with Cheddar cheese...the choices are endless.

Gruyère, piquillo pepper & basil
bread & butter pudding

- 3½ tablespoons very soft butter (for buttering the bread and greasing the dish)
- 6 slices of good white bread (approx. ½–¾ inch thick), crusts removed—about 3½ ounces prepared weight
- 3¾ ounces aged Gruyère cheese, coarsely grated (about 1 cup)
- 3 medium organic, free-range eggs
- 2 cups whole milk
- 6 ounces piquillo peppers, diced into approx. ⅓-inch cubes
- 12 basil leaves, chopped
- sea salt flakes and freshly ground black pepper

Grease a pie dish or baking dish, approx. 9½ x 6½ inches, with butter, and use the remaining butter on the slices of bread. Cut the bread into roughly 1-inch squares and arrange in the pie dish. It's really important to leave a generous space between each piece of bread to allow for expansion, so the pudding will be light and fluffy. Squash in too much bread and the end result will be disappointingly heavy. Sprinkle the grated cheese over the top.

Crack the eggs into a bowl and add the milk, chopped peppers, and basil. Whisk thoroughly for a minute or two and season well with salt and pepper.

Pour the egg and pepper mixture over the bread, then cover the dish with plastic wrap and set aside to rest in the refrigerator for a few hours for the bread to plump up, or better still overnight, if possible.

Preheat the oven to 350°F.

Bake the pudding for 40 minutes until puffed up and golden like a soufflé.

Serve with a salad of organic leaves with a perky dressing.

You'll love this curry—even ardent curry haters can't get enough of this deliciously spiced dish. It's also an excellent base for other additions, such as chunks of cooked potato.

Vegetable & tofu curry

- 2 large garlic cloves, crushed
- 1–2 chilies, seeded and roughly chopped
- zest of 1 organic lemon or 2 limes
- 3¾ ounces cilantro leaves and stalks, coarsely chopped, plus extra to serve
- ½ cup cashews, toasted and roughly chopped
- 1½ tablespoons grated fresh ginger
- 2 teaspoons ground turmeric
- 2 teaspoons ground cumin
- 4 tablespoons extra virgin olive oil
- 1 x 14-ounce can of coconut milk
- 1¾ cups homemade vegetable stock
- 18 ounces pumpkin or sweet potato, peeled and cut into ¾-inch dice
- 1 small cauliflower, weighing approx. 12 ounces, broken into small florets
- 8 ounces firm tofu, cut into approx. ¾-inch dice (about 2 cups)
- 8 ounces wax beans (green or a mixture of green and yellow)
- sea salt and freshly ground black pepper
- organic lemon or lime wedges, to serve

Combine the garlic, chili, citrus zest, roughly chopped cilantro leaves and stalks, cashews, ginger, turmeric, cumin, and 1 teaspoon of salt in a food processor and whiz to a chunky or smooth puree, depending on your preference.

Heat the olive oil in a large saucepan over medium heat, stir in the garlic and ginger puree, and cook for 3–4 minutes, stirring. Whisk in the coconut milk and stock, bring to a boil, and simmer for 8–10 minutes.

Add the chunks of sweet potato or pumpkin and return to a boil. Cover the pan with a lid and simmer for 10 minutes. Add the cauliflower florets and tofu chunks and bring back to a boil, then cover and simmer for a further 10 minutes. Add the wax beans and simmer for a further 2–3 minutes, uncovered, until all of the vegetables are cooked through.

Season with salt and pepper, and squeeze over a little lemon or lime juice, to taste. Sprinkle with lots of cilantro and serve with lemon or lime wedges.

RICE, GRAINS & PASTA

SERVES 6

This soup was inspired by a soup I ate and loved at the Little Fox in Ennistymon in County Clare. I'm not sure how they made it, but here is my interpretation, which I love. It's made in minutes, really sustaining and super-delicious.

Red lentil soup *with turmeric, masala yogurt, toasted seeds & cilantro*

- 6 tablespoons extra virgin olive oil or butter
- 8 ounces onions, chopped (about 2 cups)
- 2 teaspoons peeled and grated fresh turmeric
- 1¼ cups red lentils
- 5 cups homemade vegetable or chicken stock
- 2 teaspoons pumpkin seeds
- 2 teaspoons sunflower seeds
- 1 teaspoon each of black and white sesame seeds
- a squeeze of organic lemon juice, to taste
- sea salt flakes and freshly ground black pepper
- cilantro leaves, to garnish

FOR THE MASALA YOGURT
- 1 teaspoon coriander seeds
- 1 teaspoon cumin seeds
- 6 tablespoons plain yogurt

Heat 2 tablespoons of the extra virgin olive oil or butter in an 8½-inch/3½-quart heavy-based saucepan. Stir in the onions, then cover and sweat over gentle heat for 5–10 minutes until soft but not colored.

Add the turmeric and cook for a minute or two before stirring in the lentils. Season generously with salt and pepper. Pour in the stock, bring back to a boil, and simmer for 6–8 minutes until the lentils are soft.

Meanwhile, mix the pumpkin, sunflower, and sesame seeds in a small bowl with the remaining 4 tablespoons of oil or butter.

To make the masala yogurt, combine the cumin and coriander seeds in a mortar and grind to a fine powder. Stir into the plain yogurt in a bowl and season with salt, to taste.

Blend the soup to a coarse puree in a blender or food processor. Taste and add a squeeze of lemon juice and some more salt and pepper, if needed.

Ladle the soup into wide soup bowls, drizzle some masala yogurt over the top, and sprinkle with the seeds. Garnish with fresh cilantro leaves and serve as soon as possible.

Crunchy raw cauliflower, Romanesco, or calabrese are all delicious served raw in this fresh salad. However, to ring the changes you could drizzle the florets with oil and roast them on a baking sheet in the oven at 400°F for 15 minutes until slightly caramelized at the edges. For a vegan version of this delicious salad, omit the labneh or yogurt—it'll still be an irresistible, nutrient-dense combination.

Cauliflower, avocado, pistachio & pomegranate freekeh

- 1 pound (about 2¼ cups) freekeh
- 6 tablespoons extra virgin olive oil, plus extra to drizzle
- 3 tablespoons white wine vinegar
- 1 teaspoon ground turmeric
- 2 teaspoons honey
- 1 small cauliflower, Romanesco, or calabrese, weighing approx. 10½ ounces, divided into small florets
- 2 ripe but firm avocados, cut into chunks
- seeds from 1 small pomegranate
- 2 tablespoons nigella seeds (optional)
- 3¾ ounces pistachios, coarsely chopped (about 1 cup)
- 6–8 tablespoons labneh or thick plain yogurt
- 1–2 tablespoons sumac
- sea salt flakes and freshly ground black pepper
- lots of fresh dill sprigs, to serve

Put the freekeh into a saucepan and cover with plenty of cold water. Bring to a boil and simmer for 15–45 minutes, depending on your freekeh (broken or cracked freekeh will take 15–20 minutes, whole grains will take 35–45 minutes and will absorb more water). It should be soft but still slightly chewy. Drain, season with salt, drizzle with a little extra virgin olive oil, and toss well to coat the grains in the oil.

Meanwhile, whisk together 6 tablespoons of the extra virgin olive oil with the vinegar, turmeric, and honey in a small bowl. Drizzle over the warm freekeh and toss gently together.

Add the cauliflower florets, avocado, and some of the pomegranate seeds (save some for sprinkling) to the freekeh, and season with salt, freshly ground black pepper, and nigella seeds (if using).

To serve, pile a couple of tablespoons of the freekeh, cauliflower, and avocado salad onto a plate. Sprinkle with most of the chopped pistachios and spoon a dollop of labneh or yogurt on top. Scatter a few more pomegranate seeds, some pistachios, the sumac, and a few sprigs of dill over the labneh or yogurt and serve immediately.

This pretty vegan salad is made with lots of edible flowers from the garden. Freekeh is a Lebanese wheat that is picked while still underripe and set on fire to remove the husk, which smokes and toasts the grain. Freekeh cooking times vary quite dramatically depending on the type and age of the freekeh, so do check the package instructions. Add ricotta or feta cheese here for a non-vegan variation.

Tomato salad *with* *flowers, za'atar* & freekeh

- 3½ ounces (about ½ cup) freekeh
  or farro
- 2 tablespoons pomegranate molasses
  or moscatel vinegar
- 5 tablespoons extra virgin olive oil,
  plus extra for drizzling
- 12 cherry tomatoes
- 1 ripe but firm avocado
- 1 mini Picolino cucumber
- 2 teaspoons za'atar
- lots of edible flowers, such as violas,
  arugula flowers, borage flowers (remove
  the furry calyx from behind the flower),
  chive, or cilantro blossom
- sea salt flakes and freshly ground
  black pepper

Put the freekeh (or farro) into a saucepan and cover with plenty of cold water. Bring to a boil and simmer for 15–45 minutes, depending on the freekeh (broken or cracked freekeh will take 15–20 minutes, whole grains will take 35–45 minutes and will absorb more water). It should be soft but still slightly chewy.

Meanwhile to make the dressing, whisk the pomegranate molasses or moscatel vinegar in a little bowl with the olive oil.

When the freekeh is cooked, drain, and season well with salt and pepper. Toss with some of the dressing.

Cut the tomatoes into halves or quarters, depending on size. Peel the avocado, remove the pit and cut into 1-inch chunks. Cut the cucumber in half lengthwise, and then into thick slices at an angle.

Arrange the salad ingredients on a plate, season with salt, and drizzle with a little extra virgin olive oil. Scatter with the freekeh, drizzle over the pomegranate molasses dressing, and sprinkle with the za'atar and lots of edible flowers. Taste and add a few more flakes of sea salt if necessary and some freshly ground black pepper.

Polenta can be served the moment it's ready or it can be poured into a shallow, well-oiled dish and left to cool. It can then be sliced and chargrilled, pan-grilled, toasted or fried and served with all sorts of toppings. It can even be cut into thin slices and layered with a sauce just like lasagna. The quality of cornmeal varies so choose a really good brand. For a one-pot dish there are countless possibilities for different toppings. Just use your imagination and a little restraint.

Polenta

- 7¼ cups water
- 2 teaspoons salt
- 1½ cups coarse cornmeal (polenta flour)
- ½ cup butter
- 1–1½ cups freshly grated Parmesan
- sea salt flakes and freshly ground black pepper

Variations

GOAT CHEESE
Sprinkle the hot polenta with Gorgonzola, Cashel Blue, or goat cheese.

POLENTA WITH ARUGULA & TAPENADE
Arrange some fresh arugula leaves on the polenta and top with tapenade (olive paste).

POLENTA WITH TOMATO FONDUE & PESTO
Spread some hot Tomato Fondue (page 133) on the polenta and drizzle with a teaspoonful of your favorite pesto.

POLENTA WITH CARAMELIZED ONIONS & PESTO
Serve with some warm caramelized onions and top with a teaspoon of pesto.

Put the water into a deep, heavy-based saucepan and bring to a boil. Add salt, then sprinkle in the cornmeal very slowly, letting it slip gradually through your fingers, whisking all the time (this should take 2-3 minutes). Bring to a boil and when it starts to "erupt like a volcano" reduce the heat to the absolute minimum—use a heat diffuser mat if you have one.

Cook for about 40 minutes stirring regularly.* (I use a whisk at the beginning but as soon as the polenta comes to a boil I change to a flat wooden spoon.) The polenta is cooked when it is very thick but not solid and comes away from the sides of the pan as you stir.

As soon as the polenta is cooked, stir in the butter, freshly grated Parmesan, and lots of freshly ground pepper. Taste and add a little more salt if necessary. It should be soft and flowing; if it is a little too stiff, add some boiling water.

*If you stir constantly on a slightly higher heat, the cooking time can be reduced to about 20 minutes but it is more digestible if cooked slowly over a longer period.

Buddha bowls are delicious bowls of healthy grains, topped with fresh vegetables, fruits, herbs, seeds, and protein. This is a recipe I love but feel free to change it with the seasons. If you don't have quinoa in your pantry, you can use brown rice instead. Have fun designing your own Buddha bowl.

Smoked duck & quinoa *Buddha bowls*

- 1⅓ cups white or red quinoa
  (or a mixture)
- scant 1½ cups cold water
- 2 smoked duck breasts, thinly sliced
- 2 large nectarines or peaches,
  thinly sliced
- 2 sweet apples, finely diced and
  tossed in a little organic lemon juice
- 7 ounces cucumber or zucchini,
  finely diced (about 1¼ cups)
- 6 scallions, sliced at an angle
- 3 tablespoons pumpkin seeds, toasted
- fresh cilantro leaves, to serve

FOR THE DRESSING
- zest and juice of 2 organic limes
- 5½ tablespoons extra virgin olive oil
- 2 teaspoons toasted sesame oil
- 1 tablespoon dark soy sauce
- 1 garlic clove, crushed
- 2 tablespoons chopped chives
- 2 tablespoons chopped cilantro leaves
- 1 teaspoon honey

Tip the quinoa into a strainer and rinse under cold running water for 2–3 minutes. Place in a saucepan with the water and ½ teaspoon of salt. Bring to a boil, then cover and simmer over very low heat for 10 minutes. Remove from the heat, keeping the pan covered, and set aside for a further 10 minutes.

Meanwhile, mix all of the ingredients for the dressing together in a small bowl or jar.

Toss the warm quinoa with half of the dressing and divide between 6 serving bowls.

Arrange the sliced smoked duck breasts over the quinoa. Add the sliced nectarines, apples, and diced cucumber or zucchini—I like to place each topping in a little pile.

Drizzle over the remaining dressing and sprinkle with the scallions, toasted pumpkin seeds, and cilantro leaves.

Tuck in and enjoy.

Pearl couscous is super versatile and a great base for
a one-pot supper. Add roasted pumpkin or squash,
toasted hazelnuts, Medjool dates, arugula, mint leaves,
and maybe a little pan-grilled chicken for another
delicious combination.

Pearl couscous *with pomegranate, herbs, cranberries & cashews*

- 4 tablespoons extra virgin olive oil
- 3 cups pearl (Israeli) couscous
- 2 cups homemade chicken or
  vegetable stock
- 1 cup chopped flat-leaf parsley
- 1 cup chopped mint
- seeds from 1 pomegranate
- 3¾ ounces scallions (both white
  and green parts), chopped
  (about 1½ cups)
- ⅔ cup toasted cashews
- scant ½ cup dried cranberries
- 2 medium carrots, peeled and grated
- ½ cucumber, seeded and cut
  into ⅓-inch dice
- 1 teaspoon ground cinnamon
- 1 teaspoon ground allspice
- sea salt flakes and freshly ground
  black pepper
- cilantro and mint leaves, to serve

FOR THE DRESSING
- 3½ tablespoons extra virgin olive oil
- juice of 1 organic lemon
- 1 teaspoon honey

Heat 2 tablespoons of the extra virgin olive oil in a large
saucepan, add the couscous, and stir for 3–4 minutes
until coated and toasted. Pour in the stock, season with
½ teaspoon of salt and pepper, and bring to a boil. Cover and
simmer gently for about 10 minutes until most of the liquid
has been absorbed and the couscous is al dente. Drain, toss
in the remaining 2 tablespoons of extra virgin olive oil, and set
aside to cool.

To make the dressing, mix together the extra virgin olive oil,
freshly squeezed lemon juice, and honey.

Add the remaining ingredients to the cooled couscous and
pour over the dressing. Mix well and season with salt and
pepper. Pile into a serving dish, and scatter with the mint and
cilantro leaves.

This salad is delicious on its own but I love it with roast duck. Pumpkin or butternut squash or a mixture can be substituted for the sweet potato. Other sweet vegetables and roast bell peppers can also be used. Chickpeas or beans are another gorgeous addition.

Quinoa, sweet potato & watercress salad

- 2 large sweet potatoes, pumpkin, or butternut squash
- 3 tablespoons extra virgin olive oil
- 1 teaspoon ground coriander
- ½ teaspoon ground cinnamon
- 4 medium onions, peeled and quartered
- 1⅓ cups red or brown quinoa
- 1½ cups cold water
- 2 tablespoons toasted pumpkin seeds
- 2 tablespoons toasted sunflower seeds
- 1 tablespoon toasted sesame seeds
- 6–8 handfuls of watercress sprigs
- sea salt flakes and freshly ground black pepper

FOR THE ASIAN VINAIGRETTE
- juice and zest of 2 organic limes
- same volume of extra virgin olive oil
- 2 teaspoons toasted sesame oil
- 1 tablespoon soy sauce
- 1 garlic clove, crushed
- 1 chili, finely chopped (optional)
- 5 scallions or lots of chives, finely chopped
- lots of chopped basil or cilantro
- 1 teaspoon sugar

Preheat the oven to 450°F.

Peel the sweet potato (and seed the squash or pumpkin if using) and cut into ⅝-inch cubes. Mix the spices with the extra virgin olive oil, toss the vegetables, and spread out in an ovenproof sauté pan. Season with salt and pepper. Roast for 20–25 minutes until golden and slightly caramelized at the edges. Remove from the pan and set aside.

Rinse the quinoa in a strainer under cold water for 2–3 minutes to remove the natural bitter coating. Place it in the sauté pan with the cold water and ½ teaspoon of salt and cover with a tight-fitting lid. Bring to a boil, then reduce the heat to very low and cook, covered, for 12 minutes until the grain is tender. Remove from the heat, leave the lid on, and set aside for a further 10 minutes.

Meanwhile, make the vinaigrette. Whisk all the ingredients together in a bowl.

To serve, put the cooled quinoa, roast vegetables, and toasted seeds in a bowl. Drizzle with the vinaigrette and toss well. Season to taste. Pile onto a base of watercress sprigs and serve.

SERVES 4

Rice bowls are a brilliant way to eat a riff on chirashi sushi, one of the oldest forms. I make infinite variations on the theme—slices of duck breast, rare beef, cured fish, vegetables, scallions, pickled ginger... Just get started and this may become one of your favorite ways of eating. I love Dublin's White Mausu peanut rãyu, a delicious condiment made with peanuts, sesame, and chili flakes—a fusion of Japanese and Chinese flavors.

Lazy rice bowl *with whatever you fancy* & ponzu dressing

- 8 ounces sushi rice or aged basmati rice (about 1¼ cups)
- 1¼ cups cold water
- 1 avocado, sliced
- 3¾ ounces smoked salmon or mackerel, diced
- 2–4 scallions, cut at an angle
- 4 teaspoons diced pickled ginger
- 4 tablespoons pickled cucumber, cut into ¾-inch batons, dice, or ribbons
- 4 tablespoons White Mausu peanut rãyu, if available
- 4 tablespoons chopped cilantro
- 2 sheets of nori seaweed
- 1–2 tablespoons sesame seeds

FOR THE PONZU DRESSING
- ½ cup dark soy sauce
- finely grated zest and juice of 2 organic lemons
- finely grated zest and juice of 2 organic oranges
- 1½ teaspoons mirin
- 1 tablespoon freshly ground black pepper
- 1 tablespoon finely chopped shallot

First prepare the sushi rice. Rinse the rice for 10 minutes in a colander or strainer under cold running water or until the water becomes clear. Tip the rice into a saucepan, cover with the water, and set aside for 30–45 minutes to "wake up the rice."

Bring the rice to a boil and simmer for 10 minutes until all the water has been absorbed. Avoid the temptation to stir the rice or remove the lid. Increase the heat right at the end for the last 10 seconds, just before you turn off the heat. Remove the lid, place a dish towel over the rice and replace the lid. Set aside for 20 minutes.

Meanwhile, make the dressing. Whiz all the ingredients together in a blender. Season to taste.

Fill each bowl over half-full with sushi rice and top with the avocado, smoked salmon, scallions, pickled ginger, and pickled cucumber. Add a dollop of peanut rãyu, if available. Sprinkle over some cilantro, the crumbled nori seaweed, and sesame seeds. Serve drizzled with the ponzu dressing.

Pearl barley is super nutritious, absolutely delicious, and very versatile. I love to cook it as a pilaf and enjoy adding extra bits and pieces, depending on the season— sweet cherry tomatoes, crisp cucumber dice, roast squash or pumpkin, peas, fava beans, Romanesco or broccoli florets, spinach or kale all work well.

Pearl barley pilaf
with greens & walnuts

- 3 tablespoons butter or olive oil
- 8 ounces echalion (banana) shallots, peeled and diced (about 1½ cups)
- 2½ cups pearl barley
- 7¾ cups homemade chicken stock
- 7 ounces watercress (or arugula or sorrel), chopped
- ⅓ cup coarsely chopped walnuts
- freshly squeezed organic lemon juice
- sea salt flakes and freshly ground black pepper

Melt the butter in a deep saucepan over gentle heat, add the shallots, and cook for 2–3 minutes until just starting to soften. Add the pearl barley and toss the grains in the butter. Season with salt and pepper. Pour in the stock and bring to a boil, then cover and simmer gently for 45 minutes–1 hour until the pearl barley is fully cooked.

You now have a platform to add lots of delicious extras: here I've added chopped watercress leaves. Stir in the chopped watercress and allow it to wilt for 2–3 minutes, then add the coarsely chopped walnuts and some freshly squeezed lemon juice. Season to taste and serve.

I can't tell you how many times this soda bread pizza base has come to the rescue when I needed to whip up a dish of something filling and delicious in no time at all. It can be as simple as a topping of grated aged Cheddar cheese or halved, well-seasoned cherry tomatoes.

Soda bread pizza
with delicious toppings

- scant 3½ cups all-purpose flour, plus extra for kneading and rolling
- 1 teaspoon baking soda
- 1 teaspoon sea salt
- 1½–1¾ cups buttermilk
- extra virgin olive oil, for brushing
- ½–1 tablespoon chopped rosemary
- 1¾ ounces chorizo, sliced
- 12 ounces Tomato Fondue (page 133) or chopped fresh or canned tomatoes mixed with seasoning/spices
- 8 bocconcini, halved
- scant ¼ cup grated Parmesan cheese
- lots of snipped flat-leaf parsley

Fully preheat the oven to 450°F.

Sift the flour, baking soda, and salt into a large bowl. Make a well in the center. Pour in 1½ cups of the buttermilk and, using one hand, mix in the flour from the sides of the bowl. Mix to a softish, not too wet and sticky consistency, adding more buttermilk if necessary. When it all comes together, turn out the dough onto a floured board, knead lightly for a few seconds, tidy it up and flip it over.

Brush a roasting pan, approx. 12 x 9 x 2 inches, with olive oil. Roll out the dough lightly to fit the pan and sprinkle with rosemary. Scatter the sliced chorizo evenly over the surface. Spread a layer of tomato fondue over the chorizo and arrange some halved bocconcini on top. Sprinkle over the Parmesan.

Transfer the pan to the fully preheated oven on a low rack and bake for an initial 15 minutes. Then reduce the heat to 400°F and bake for a further 20–25 minutes or until the dough is cooked and it's golden and bubbling on top.

Sprinkle with the parsley and serve with a good green salad.

Other tasty toppings

'NDUJA AND BOCCONCINI

Follow the main recipe, omitting the rosemary and replacing the chorizo with 4½ ounces 'nduja. Sprinkle with fresh marjoram to serve.

PESTO & PARMESAN

Follow the main recipe, omitting the rosemary and chorizo and replacing the tomato fondue with 3 tablespoons of loose basil or wild garlic pesto. Top with 1–1¼ cups grated mozzarella or 1–1¼ cups soft goat cheese and scant ¼ cup grated Parmesan.

TAPENADE & SOFT GOAT CHEESE

Follow the main recipe, omitting the rosemary and chorizo and replacing the tomato fondue with 3 tablespoons of olive tapenade, and the mozzarella with 1–1¼ cups of soft goat cheese.

SPICED EGGPLANT

Follow the main recipe, omitting the rosemary and chorizo and replacing with 6–8 tablespoons of Spiced Eggplant (page 118).

CHEDDAR CHEESE & SCALLION

Follow the main recipe, omitting the chorizo and replacing the rosemary with 4 tablespoons of sliced scallions and the Parmesan with 1 cup of grated aged Cheddar cheese.

I first tasted this dish at The Bangala in Karaikudi in South India. It's one of my favorite comfort foods. Serve alone or as an accompaniment to chicken or fish. I love to sprinkle some sprigs of chervil on top—not traditional, but delicious.

Chettinad tomato rice

- scant ½ cup extra virgin olive oil
- scant ½ cup ghee or clarified butter (page 16)
- 1 x 2-inch cinnamon stick
- 4 green cardamom pods
- 2 bay leaves
- 2 onions, finely chopped
- 1–2 green chilies, halved
- 3 large ripe tomatoes, weighing approx. 10½ ounces, peeled (see page 112) and minced (like a thick puree)
- 3 cups basmati rice, soaked for 15–30 minutes in cold water and drained
- 3¾ cups homemade chicken stock or water
- scant 1 cup coconut milk
- 1½ teaspoons sea salt, to taste
- ½ teaspoon ground turmeric
- chervil sprigs (optional), to serve

Heat a deep saucepan over medium heat. Add the oil and ghee or clarified butter. Add the cinnamon, cardamom, and bay leaves, followed by the onions and green chilies. Sauté for 3–4 minutes until all the ingredients turn a pale golden color.

Add the tomatoes and stir for 3–4 minutes. Add the soaked and drained rice, chicken stock or water, coconut milk, salt, and turmeric. Bring to a boil and cover with a lid. Cook over gentle heat for about 10 minutes until the rice is cooked and all of the liquid has been absorbed. The rice will happily sit for 15–20 minutes off the heat, but I like to serve it immediately with lots of chervil sprigs on top.

What sweet agony to have to choose just one risotto for each season, when there are so many good things to embellish the already gorgeous classic. Master the basic recipe and remember the secret is to source the best-quality rice you can—carnaroli, vilano nano, or a good arborio—and to have a delicious chicken, fish, or vegetable broth for the base with plenty of flavor. Freshly grated Parmesan is another essential—don't forget to stir in a nice dollop of butter just before serving.

A risotto
for all seasons

FOR A CLASSIC RISOTTO
- 2 tablespoons extra virgin olive oil
- 3½ tablespoons butter
- 1 medium onion, finely chopped
- generous 2 cups best-quality risotto rice, such as carnaroli, arborio, or vilano nano
- 4¼–5½ cups hot broth or homemade chicken or vegetable stock
- ⅔ cup freshly grated Parmesan cheese
- sea salt flakes

Melt the oil and half the butter in a 10½-inch heavy-based saucepan. Add the onion and sweat over gentle heat for 5–10 minutes until soft but not colored.

Add the rice and stir until well coated. Cook for a minute or so and then add scant ⅔ cup of the broth. Continue to cook, stirring continuously, until all of the liquid has been absorbed, before adding another scant ⅔ cup of broth. The heat should be brisk, but on the other hand if it's too hot the rice will be soft outside but still chewy inside. If it's too slow, the rice will be gluey. It's difficult to know which is worse, so the trick is to regulate the heat so that the rice bubbles continuously. The risotto should take about 25–30 minutes in total to cook: when it has been cooking for about 20 minutes, add the broth more gradually, only about 4 tablespoons (¼ cup) at a time. I use a small ladle. Watch the rice very carefully from there on. The risotto is done when the rice is cooked, but still ever so slightly "al dente." It should be soft and creamy and quite loose, rather than thick. The moment you are happy with the texture, stir in the remaining butter and Parmesan cheese, taste, and add more salt if necessary. Risotto does not benefit from hanging around—the texture should be soft and flowing.

For spring risotto, fold the chopped watercress or wild garlic into the risotto right at the end, just before you add the butter and Parmesan.

Variations

SPRING RISOTTO
WITH WATERCRESS
- 8 ounces wild watercress sprigs, chopped, or 8 ounces wild garlic, chopped

SUMMER RISOTTO WITH
FAVA BEANS
- 1 pound (about 3½ cups) fava beans, blanched
- 2 handfuls of fava bean shoots
- a few fava bean flowers, if available, to garnish

AUTUMN RISOTTO WITH ROOTS
- 5½ ounces carrots, peeled
- 5½ ounces beets, peeled
- 1¾ tablespoons butter
- ¼ teaspoon chili flakes (optional)
- 3½ ounces chopped kale
- a few sprigs of chervil, to garnish

WINTER RISOTTO WITH
RADICCHIO OR BELGIAN ENDIVE
- 1 head radicchio or red Belgian endive
- ½ cup coarsely chopped walnuts
- 3¾ ounces blue cheese, such as Crozier Blue, Dolcelatte, or your favorite blue (optional)

For summer risotto, mix in the blanched fava beans and bean shoots right at the end, just before you add the butter and Parmesan. Garnish with a few fava bean flowers, if available.

For autumn risotto, chop the peeled carrots and beets into ¾-inch dice. Sweat the dice in 1¾ tablespoons butter for 8–10 minutes—the length of time will depend on the age of the beets and carrots—then remove from the pan before the onion is sweated. Add the cooked carrot and beet to the risotto halfway through the cooking time. Add the chili flakes when the onion is cooked (if you wish). Just before the end of cooking, add the kale. Garnish with a few sprigs of chervil.

For a winter risotto, make up the risotto in the classic recipe, substituting the broth or stock with 50/50 red wine and stock (optional). Break the radicchio or Belgian endive into small bite-size pieces and fold in close to the end, just before you add the butter and Parmesan. Scatter over the walnuts and add a dollop of blue cheese, if you wish.

For those of you who are conditioned to cook pasta in a huge pan of boiling salted water, the idea of cooking pasta in the sauce in just one pot may be quite a stretch to consider attempting, but do try it. The starch from the pasta thickens the sauce and the pasta absorbs the flavors deliciously; it's a revelation and you'll have such fun experimenting. For some reason I still feel slightly guilty, but less washing up helps to salve my conscience. You'll need considerably more liquid than in a regular pasta sauce because the pasta will absorb much of the liquid.

One-pot pasta *with tomato & chorizo*

- 2 tablespoons extra virgin olive oil
- 1 medium onion, sliced
- 1 garlic clove, crushed
- ½–1 red chili, chopped
- 2 pounds very ripe tomatoes, peeled (see page 112), in summer, or 2½ x 14-ounce cans of plum tomatoes in winter
- zest of 1 organic lemon
- 1–2 teaspoons chopped rosemary, depending on the strength of flavor
- 8 ounces chorizo, peeled and diced (about 1¾ cups)
- generous 3½ cups homemade chicken or vegetable stock
- scant ¾ cup heavy cream
- 10½–12 ounces fettuccine or spaghetti
- 2 tablespoons chopped flat-leaf parsley
- scant ½ cup freshly grated Parmesan
- sea salt flakes, freshly ground black pepper, and a generous pinch of sugar, to taste

Heat the oil in a 6-quart stainless-steel saucepan. Add the onions and garlic, toss until coated, cover, and sweat over gentle heat until soft but not colored. Add the chili. It is vital for the success of this dish that the onions are completely soft before the tomatoes are added.

Slice the fresh or canned tomatoes and add to the onions with all the juices and the lemon zest. Season with salt, pepper, and sugar (canned tomatoes need lots of sugar because of their high acidity). Add the rosemary and cook, uncovered, for a further 10 minutes, or until the tomato softens. Cook fresh tomatoes for a shorter time to preserve the lively fresh flavor.

Add the chorizo, stock, and cream. Bring back to a boil, add the pasta, and stir gently to separate the strands and prevent sticking. Return to a boil, cover and simmer for 4 minutes, then let sit in the tightly covered saucepan for a further 4–5 minutes, or until just al dente. When you add the dried pasta, it will seem too much, but hold your nerve; it will soften within a minute or two and cook deliciously in the sauce.

Season to taste and sprinkle with lots of chopped parsley and grated Parmesan. Serve.

As you can imagine, you can vary the fish and shellfish here depending on what's freshest and best—scallops would be a super-luxurious option and even a little smoked fish is delicious.

One-pot pasta *with* shrimp, monkfish, mussels & dill

- 2 tablespoons extra virgin olive oil
- 1 medium onion, sliced
- 1 garlic clove, crushed
- ½–1 red chili, chopped
- 2 pounds very ripe tomatoes, peeled (see page 112), in summer, or 2½ x 14-ounce cans of plum tomatoes in winter
- zest of 1 organic lemon
- 1 teaspoon roasted and coarsely ground fennel seeds
- generous 3½ cups homemade fish, chicken, or vegetable stock
- scant ¾ cup heavy cream
- 10½–12 ounces fettuccine or spaghetti
- 1 pound monkfish tail, cut into ¾-inch dice
- 2¼ pounds mussels in their shells, washed but not debearded before cooking
- 3¾ ounces peeled and cooked shrimps
- 2 tablespoons chopped flat-leaf parsley
- 2 tablespoons chopped dill
- scant ½ cup finely grated Parmesan
- sea salt flakes, freshly ground black pepper, and a generous pinch of sugar, to taste

Heat the oil in a 6-quart stainless-steel saucepan, add the onions and garlic, and toss until coated. Cover the pan with a lid and sweat over gentle heat until the onions are soft but not colored. Add the chili. It is vital that the onions are completely soft before you add the tomatoes.

Slice the fresh or canned tomatoes and add to the pan with all the juices. Stir in the lemon zest and fennel seeds, and season to taste with salt, pepper, and sugar (canned tomatoes need lots of sugar because of their high acidity). Cook for a further 10 minutes, uncovered, or until the tomato softens. Cook fresh tomatoes for a shorter time to preserve their fresh lively flavor.

Add the stock and the cream, and bring back to a boil. Add the pasta, stirring gently to prevent it from sticking. Season again. Return the sauce to a boil, then cover and simmer for 4 minutes. Bring the sauce back a boil, and then add the monkfish and mussels. Cover the pan with a tight-fitting lid and set aside, off the heat, for a further 2–3 minutes until the monkfish turns opaque and the mussels open. Carefully stir in the cooked peeled shrimp and heat through for 1–2 minutes. Test the pasta, it should be al dente.

Season to taste and scatter with lots of chopped parsley and dill, and a sprinkling of Parmesan. Serve.

Have you ever tried cooking your spaghetti bolognaise in just one pot? It's a revelation—and much less work when it comes to doing the dishes!

Spaghetti
bolognaise-ish

- 2 tablespoons extra virgin olive oil
- 4 ounces bacon lardons (about ½ cup)
- 1 medium onion, sliced
- 1 garlic clove, crushed
- ½–1 red chili, chopped
- 2 pounds very ripe tomatoes, peeled (see page 112), in summer, or 2½ x 14-ounce cans of plum tomatoes in winter
- 1–2 teaspoons ground cumin
- 2 tablespoons freshly chopped herbs, such as thyme, flat-leaf parsley, tarragon, or rosemary (or a mixture)
- 3 cups organic ground beef, seasoned
- generous 3½ cups homemade chicken or beef stock
- 10½–12 ounces spaghetti
- 2 tablespoons chopped flat-leaf parsley
- scant ½ cup finely grated Parmesan
- sea salt flakes, freshly ground black pepper, and a generous pinch of sugar, to taste

Heat the oil in a 6-quart stainless steel saucepan and add the bacon lardons. Stir and cook for 3–4 minutes before adding the onions and garlic. Toss until well coated. Cover the pan with a lid and sweat over gentle heat until the onion is soft but not colored. Add the chili. It is vital for the success of this dish that the onions are completely soft before the tomatoes are added.

Slice the fresh or canned tomatoes and add to the pan with all the juices. Season with salt, pepper, and sugar (canned tomatoes need lots of sugar because of their high acidity). Stir in the cumin and fresh herbs. Bring to a boil, then reduce the heat and simmer, uncovered, for just 10 minutes until the tomatoes soften. Cook fresh tomatoes for a shorter time to preserve their fresh lively flavor.

Crumble in the well-seasoned ground beef, stir, and cook for 3–4 minutes. Pour in the stock and return to a boil, then add the spaghetti, stirring gently to separate the strands. Return the sauce to a boil, then cover the pan with a lid and simmer for 4–5 minutes or until the pasta is al dente.

Season to taste and scatter with lots of chopped parsley and Parmesan. Serve.

Try this fun way to cook pasta—all in one pot.
Sounds like sacrilege, but it works brilliantly.

One-pot *mushroom* pasta

- 2 tablespoons butter
- 3 ounces onion, finely chopped
  (about ¾ cup)
- 8 ounces flat mushrooms, sliced
  (about 3¾–4 cups)
- a squeeze of organic lemon juice
- 3 tablespoons chopped flat-leaf parsley
- 1 teaspoon thyme leaves
- ½ tablespoon chopped chives
- 2 tablespoons chopped marjoram
- 3¾ cups homemade vegetable or
  chicken stock
- ½ cup heavy cream
- 10½–14 ounces fettuccine or spaghetti
- scant ½ cup freshly grated Parmesan
- sea salt flakes and freshly ground
  black pepper

Melt the butter in a 10-inch/3-quart casserole until it foams. Stir in the onion, cover with a lid, and sweat over gentle heat for 5–10 minutes until soft but not colored. Remove the onion to a bowl.

Cook the sliced mushrooms in the hot casserole, in batches if necessary. Season each batch with salt, pepper, and a tiny squeeze of lemon juice. Add the onion back to the pan, together with 1 tablespoon of the parsley and the thyme. Pour in the stock and cream, bring to a boil, and simmer for 3–4 minutes. Season to taste.

Add the pasta, stirring to separate the strands and prevent it from sticking, and boil for 4 minutes. Then turn off the heat and allow the pasta to stand, tightly covered with a lid, for 4–5 minutes or until it is al dente.

Sprinkle with the remaining parsley and the grated Parmesan. Taste and add a little more lemon juice, if necessary. Serve.

SWEET THINGS

Clafoutis is a sort of fluffy custard, a base for whatever seasonal fruit you can lay your hands on: rhubarb or gooseberries are delicious, but you need to adjust the sugar. This one is made with pit-in damsons, or you can use Mirabelle plums. I often have rose geranium or mint sugar in a jar—this also makes a delicious sprinkle.

Damson clafoutis

- 1 tablespoon softened butter, for greasing
- 5 organic, free-range eggs
- scant ½ cup superfine sugar
- ½ cup plus 1 tablespoon all-purpose flour
- scant ½ cup heavy cream
- 1¾ cups plus 1 tablespoon whole milk
- ½ teaspoon ground cinnamon
  or ½ teaspoon pure vanilla extract
- 1 pound 10 ounces damsons or Mirabelle
  plums, or cherries, peaches, nectarines,
  or greengages, in season
- ¼ cup coarsely chopped pistachios
  or sliced almonds
- powdered or superfine sugar, to sprinkle
- softly whipped cream, to serve

Preheat the oven to 350°F and grease a 11¼-inch round baking dish or similar with softened butter.

Whisk the eggs with the superfine sugar in a mixing bowl. Sift in the flour, pour in the cream and milk, and add the cinnamon or vanilla extract. Whisk together to form a smooth batter with no lumps.

Pour half the batter into the buttered dish. Scatter the damsons or Mirabelle plums on top. (I leave the pits in, but you could pit them if you wish. If using cherries or greengages, you can scatter them over whole, or pit them if you prefer; peaches or nectarines are best halved or quartered, depending on size.) Pour the remaining batter over the fruit.

Bake for 30–40 minutes, and then scatter with the chopped pistachios or sliced almonds and continue to cook for a further 10 minutes until the clafoutis is puffed up and the nuts are golden. Sprinkle with powdered or superfine sugar, to serve. Accompany with lots of softly whipped cream.

Many pears need a little help from aromatic herbs or spices to enhance their flavor. This recipe for poached pears infused in basil syrup is a wonderful dessert—and I've also included lots of variations for you to try once you've mastered the basic method.

Poached pears *with basil syrup*

- 1 cup sugar
- 2 cups water
- 6–8 basil leaves
- 3 tablespoons freshly squeezed organic lemon juice
- 4 firm pears, such as Conference, Doyenne du Comice, or Bartlett

Variations

POACHED PEARS WITH SAFFRON SYRUP
Replace the basil with 6 lightly crushed whole cardamom pods and ¼ teaspoon of good-quality saffron threads.

LEMON POACHED PEARS
Replace the basil with the thinly pared zest and juice of 1 organic lemon.

SWEET GERANIUM POACHED PEARS
Replace the basil with 3–4 large sweet geranium leaves (*Pelargonium graveolens*).

LEMON VERBENA POACHED PEARS
Replace the basil with 4–6 lemon verbena leaves.

GINGER POACHED PEARS
Replace the basil with a 1-inch piece of fresh ginger, cut into thin slivers.

Put the sugar, water, basil, and lemon juice into 13-inch stainless-steel sauté pan and stir over gentle heat to dissolve the sugar. Bring to a simmer.

Meanwhile, start on the pears. Peel, halve, and core the pears, leaving the stalks intact, and as you finish each one pop it into the simmering syrup, cut-side up. Cover the surface of the pan with a parchment-paper lid to prevent the cut surface from discoloring, then pop on the lid of the pan, and cook gently for 20–30 minutes, spooning the syrup over the pears every now and then.

Carefully remove the pears and arrange them in a serving dish in a single layer, cut-side down. Taste the syrup and, if necessary, simmer over gentle heat with the lid off for a few minutes to concentrate the flavor. Be careful not to cook it for too long, or the syrup will caramelize.

Remove the basil and pour the syrup over the pears then set aside to cool. Serve chilled.

The poached pears will keep for several weeks, covered, in the refrigerator.

This is definitely my "go-to" recipe for a super quick and delicious comfort pud. Even though I call this version with plums Autumn Tart, I make it throughout the year with different fruits, including rhubarb, gooseberries, greengages, peaches, nectarines, apples, and pears, and add a few juicy fresh berries when I have them. The sponge base is quick to make in a food processor and you can ring the changes by experimenting with different flavors, such as freshly chopped lemon verbena, rose geranium, or rosemary.

Autumn tart

FOR THE FRUIT BASE
- ¾ cup plus 2 tablespoons sugar
- 7½ tablespoons water
- 1 pound plums, halved and pitted, or baking apples (such as Granny Smiths or Pink Lady), peeled and cut into quarters or eighths, depending on size

FOR THE SPONGE TOPPING
- ⅔ cup softened butter
- ¾ cup sugar
- 1½ cups self-rising flour
- 3 organic, free-range eggs

Preheat the oven to 315°F.

Put the sugar and water into a 10-inch ovenproof sauté pan or cast-iron frying pan and stir over medium heat until the sugar has dissolved. Continue to cook, without stirring, until the sugar caramelizes to a rich golden brown (if the caramel is not dark enough, the tart will be too sweet).

Once the caramel darkens to a golden brown, remove the pan from the heat and arrange the prepared fruit, cut-side down, in a single layer over the caramel.

To make the sponge topping, combine the butter, sugar, and flour in the bowl of a food processor. Whiz for a second or two, then add the eggs and stop as soon as the mixture comes together. Spoon the cake mixture over the plums and spread gently to create an even layer.

Bake for about 1 hour. The center should be firm to the touch and the edges slightly shrunk from the sides of the pan.

Remove from the oven and set aside to rest in the pan for 4–5 minutes before turning out. Serve with crème fraîche or softly whipped cream.

Variations

ROAST APPLES WITH CINNAMON SUGAR

Add 1 teaspoon of ground cinnamon to the sugar.

ROAST APPLES WITH GOLDEN RAISINS & HAZELNUTS

Add 1 scant teaspoon of golden raisins and 1 teaspoon of coarsely chopped toasted hazelnuts to the sugar for each apple. Top each apple with a tiny dollop of butter.

Don't forget this simple recipe for a much-loved fall or winter dessert—a great way to use up any last windfall cooking apples. I love to roast them in an enamel roasting pan. For a special dish, you could vary the fillings and allow your guests to select their favorite. Brown sugar and cream is a compulsory accompaniment. Nowadays, baked apples are often stuffed with "exciting" mixtures which may include dried fruit, lemon zest, nuts, and spices. This is nice occasionally, but my favorite is still the simple roast apple of my childhood. It's important to note that the apples will cook much faster in the fall than they will later on in the year, when they will have most probably come from a cold store.

A *tray of* roast apples

- 9 large cooking apples, preferably Bramley
- 9 tablespoons sugar
- 1¾ tablespoons butter
- ½ cup plus 2 tablespoons water
- softly whipped cream and dark brown sugar, to serve

MARZIPAN ROAST APPLES

Fill the apple cavities with 8 ounces (about ¾ cup) marzipan mixed with ½ teaspoon of ground cinnamon.

ROAST APPLES WITH PEDRO XIMENEZ RAISINS

Soak ¾ cup raisins in warm Pedro Ximenez sherry for at least 30 minutes, or better still overnight. Combine the raisins with 4 tablespoons of superfine sugar and use to fill the apples. Top with butter and bake as above. Serve with scant 1 cup softly whipped cream mixed with 3 tablespoons of Pedro Ximenez.

Preheat the oven to 350°F.

Core the apples and score the skin of each around the equator. Arrange the apples in a single layer in a baking dish large enough to take the apples in a single layer, approx. 12 x 10 x 2 inches, and for the simplest but nonetheless totally delicious version, fill the center of each one with 1 generous tablespoon sugar. Put a little dab of butter on top of each.

Pour a little water around the apples and roast in the oven for about 1 hour. They should be fluffy and burst slightly when they are fully cooked, but still be fat and puffy (not totally collapsed). Serve as soon as possible with softly whipped cream and brown sugar.

Roasting a stone fruit is a simple, easy way to rustle up a delicious dessert. I like to vary the fresh herbs and flavorings from season to season, to include lemon thyme, marjoram, or lemon verbena, which all add a bit of magic. This version is extra gorgeous with homemade vanilla or honey and lavender ice cream.

Roast peaches, nectarines, or apricots *with honey & lavender*

- 8 peaches, nectarines, or apricots, halved and pitted
- 2 tablespoons honey
- 2 tablespoons freshly squeezed organic lemon juice
- 1¾ tablespoons butter
- 1–2 teaspoons dried lavender buds

TO SERVE
- a few fresh lavender flowers (if available)
- softly whipped cream or crème fraîche

Preheat the oven to 500°F.

Arrange the prepared fruit, cut-side down, in a single layer in a baking dish approx. 12 x 10 x 2 inches and drizzle with the honey. Squeeze over the lemon juice and put a little dab of butter on each piece of fruit. Sprinkle with the dried lavender and roast for 8–10 minutes.

Serve warm, sprinkled with a few lavender flowers (if available) and accompanied by homemade vanilla or honey and lavender ice cream, or softly whipped cream or crème fraîche.

French toast is so good that you can almost forget how economical it is. It is a brilliant way to use up leftover bread or brioche that might otherwise be wasted. Every country has its own version of this simple dish. I've eaten variations from India to the UK, where it's also called knights of Windsor, or poor knights, or eggy bread. Then there's German toast, known as gypsy toast, torrija in Spain, Bombay toast, and, of course, the French classic pain perdu. It's actually better if the bread is a little stale. You may want to add a little vanilla extract to the batter when serving a sweet version and a dash of cream. Make individual toasts or cover the whole base of the pan with a pain perdu for sharing.

Pain perdu

- 3 organic, free-range eggs
- scant ¾ cup whole milk
- a tiny pinch of salt
- 6 slices of white bread or brioche
- 4 tablespoons butter (clarified butter is best—see page 16)
- fresh berries and powdered sugar, to serve

Whisk the eggs, milk, and salt together in a bowl until well blended. Strain the mixture into a shallow bowl in which you can easily soak the bread. Dip both sides of each slice of bread or brioche in the batter.

Melt 2 tablespoons of the butter in a frying pan. Fry the bread over medium heat until very lightly browned, turning once. Repeat with the remaining bread and butter. Serve warm with fresh berries and a generous sprinkling of powdered sugar.

Tasty toppings

Serve with sliced and sugared strawberries, raspberries, and/or blueberries, mascarpone, and lots of shredded mint.

Serve with a dollop of sweet applesauce and a dusting of ground cinnamon.

Serve with sliced banana, a dollop of chilled plain yogurt, some roughly chopped walnuts, and maple syrup.

Variations

SPICED FRENCH TOAST
Add ½ teaspoon of ground cinnamon or nutmeg to the batter.

FOR CITRUS FRENCH TOAST
Add 2 teaspoons of grated organic lemon or orange zest to the batter.

A dish of roasted fruit couldn't be simpler—rhubarb, plums, greengages, apricots, peaches, apples, or pears. I love to add some freshly chopped herbs, such as rose geranium or lemon verbena to the sugar or the accompanying cream. I've become a huge fan of the sweet and intense flavor of roast rhubarb.

Roast rhubarb

- 2¼ pounds red rhubarb
- 1–1¼ cups sugar
- 2–3 teaspoons freshly chopped herbs, such as rose geranium or lemon verbena (optional)
- ice cream, labneh, or thick Jersey or heavy cream, to serve

Trim the rhubarb stalks if necessary. Slice the rhubarb into 1-inch pieces and arrange in a single layer in an 18 x 12-inch nonreactive baking dish. Scatter the sugar over the rhubarb and let macerate for 1 hour or more, until the juices start to run.

Preheat the oven to 400°F.

Cover the rhubarb with a sheet of parchment paper and roast in the oven for 10–20 minutes, depending on the thickness of the stalks, until the rhubarb is just tender. Keep a close eye on the rhubarb as it can disintegrate very quickly

Serve hot or cold with ice cream, labneh, or thick cream.

SERVES 6

This is a superb recipe—a one-pot compote with an intense flavor—which keeps brilliantly in the refrigerator for a week or more.

Myrtle's compote of pears

- 6 ripe pears
- ½ cup plus 1 tablespoon sugar
- 1 organic lemon

Halve the pears, peel thinly, and core carefully, keeping a good shape. Put them in a pan that will just fit them nicely. Add the sugar, a few thin strips of lemon zest, and the lemon juice. Cover with a well-fitting lid and cook gently for 20–30 minutes until soft. Cool and serve alone or with softly whipped cream.

You'll find yourself reaching for this recipe over and over again. Here I use apple and blackberries with sweet geranium, but I also love it with green gooseberries and elderflower, or plums. I enjoy arranging the blackberries and apples in neat lines, but if you are super busy just sprinkle them over the top of the sponge base.

Apple & blackberry traybake
with sweet geranium sugar

- 8–12 lemon geranium leaves
  (*Pelargonium graveolens*)
- 3–4 cooking apples,
  such as Bramleys
- generous 1 cup blackberries
- scant 6 tablespoons superfine sugar
- crème fraîche or softly whipped
  cream, to serve

FOR THE SPONGE BASE
- 1 cup softened butter
- ¾ cup superfine sugar
- 2 cups self-rising flour
- 4 organic, free-range eggs

Preheat the oven to 315°F.

Line the base of a 13 x 9 x 2-inch cake pan, or a 10-inch sauté pan or cast-iron frying pan with parchment paper, allowing it to hang over the sides. Arrange 6–8 sweet geranium leaves over the base—these give the sponge a delicate lemony flavor.

To make the sponge base, combine the butter, sugar, and flour in the bowl of a food processor. Whiz for a second or two, then add the eggs and stop as soon as the mixture comes together. Spoon the mixture over the base of the pan as evenly as possible (over the sweet geranium leaves).

Peel the apples. Cut into thin slices and arrange on top of the sponge in three lines. Arrange a line of blackberries in between each row. Sprinkle 2 tablespoons of the superfine sugar over the top and bake for about 50 minutes.

Meanwhile, whiz 2–4 sweet geranium leaves with the remaining 4 tablespoons superfine sugar in a food processor. Spread over a baking sheet and set aside at room temperature to dry out.

Once it is fully cooked, the center of the cake should be firm to the touch and the edges slightly shrunk from the sides of the pan. Serve in the pan, sprinkled with the sweet geranium sugar. Alternatively, let rest in the pan for 4–5 minutes before turning out. Serve with crème fraîche or softly whipped cream.

These are made in minutes and are pretty irresistible. If you want to ring the changes, try one of the equally delicious variations listed below. The dry ingredients may be weighed up ahead—even the day before. You can rub in the butter in advance, but do not add the rising agent and liquid until just before cooking.

Sticky orange swirls

- ⅓ cup cold butter, plus extra for greasing
- scant 3½ cups all-purpose flour
- a pinch of salt
- 1½ teaspoons baking powder
- 2 tablespoons superfine sugar
- zest of 1 organic orange
- 2 small organic, free-range eggs
- ¾ cup plus 2 tablespoons whole milk
- egg wash, made by beating
  1 small organic, free-range egg
  with 2 teaspoons milk
- 2 tablespoons turbinado sugar

FOR THE ORANGE BUTTER
- ⅓ cup softened butter
- 1½ teaspoons finely grated organic
  orange zest
- ¾ cup powdered sugar

Preheat the oven to 500°F and grease a 13 x 9 x 2-inch cake pan with a little butter.

First make the orange butter. Cream the butter with the orange zest. Add the powdered sugar and beat until fluffy. Set aside.

Sift the flour into a large wide bowl, add a pinch of salt, the baking powder, and the superfine sugar. Finely grate the zest of the orange into the bowl. Mix the dry ingredients together with your hands, to incorporate as much as air as possible.

Cut the cold butter into cubes or grate coarsely and toss well in the flour. Using the tips of your fingers, rub in the butter until the mixture resembles large flakes. Make a well in the center. Whisk the eggs with the milk in a cup and pour all at once into the well. Using the fingers of your "best hand" outstretched and stiff, combine the ingredients in a full circular movement from the center to the outside of the bowl.

Sprinkle some flour on your work surface and turn out the dough. Tidy around the edges of the dough, then flip it over and roll or pat it gently into a 12 x 8-inch rectangle about ¾-inch thick.

Slather most of the soft orange butter evenly over the dough, then roll it up tightly from the long side. Divide into four quarters, and then cut each piece into three to give you 12 pieces altogether. Brush the cut side of each swirl with the egg wash and dip in the turbinado sugar. Arrange side by side in the buttered roasting pan, leaving a little room for expansion. Bake for 10 minutes.

Serve while still warm, or at room temperature, with a little extra orange butter. Pull apart gently like a tear and share.

This dessert can be made ahead and enjoyed
warm or cold. Rosewater varies in strength so
be careful to add gradually and taste as you go.

Kheer marwadi
Indian rice pudding

Variations

CHOCOLATE & HAZELNUT SWIRLS

Make the dough and roll out into a
rectangle about ¾ inch thick. Slather
with 6–8 tablespoons of chocolate and
hazelnut spread, then roll up lengthwise
like a jelly roll and cut into 12 pieces.
Brush the cut side of each swirl with
egg wash and sprinkle with coarsely
chopped toasted hazelnuts. Bake for
10–12 minutes.

MARMALADE SCONES

Make the dough as before and roll out into
a ¾-inch-thick rectangle. Slather with
6–8 tablespoons of marmalade (chop the
peel finely first), then roll up lengthwise
like a jelly roll and cut into 12 pieces. Brush
the cut side of each swirl with egg wash
and bake for 10–12 minutes.

CINNAMON BUTTER SCONES

Make the dough and roll out into a
¾-inch-thick rectangle. To make the
cinnamon butter, cream together ⅔ cup
softened butter, 1¼ cups light brown
sugar, and 1 tablespoon of ground
cinnamon. Slather the cinnamon butter
over the dough, roll up lengthwise like a
jelly roll and cut into 12 pieces. Brush the
cut side of each swirl with egg wash. Mix
2 tablespoons granulated or turbinado
sugar with 1 teaspoon of ground
cinnamon and sprinkle over the surface.
Bake for 10 minutes.

- 1 tablespoon coconut oil
- generous ¼ cup basmati rice, soaked
  for 1 hour in cold water and drained
- 4¼ cups coconut milk
- 2 cups water
- 3 tablespoons whole almonds,
  skinned and chopped very finely or
  ground to a paste
- ½ cup sugar
- ¾ cup grated fresh coconut
- 2½ tablespoons raisins
- scant ½ cup pistachios, cut into slivers
- scant ½ cup blanched almonds,
  cut into slivers
- ½ teaspoon ground seeds from green
  cardamom pods
- 2 teaspoons kewra extract or
  rosewater, to taste
- chopped pistachios and rose petals
  (if available), to serve

Heat the coconut oil in a pan. Add the soaked and drained
rice and stir for 2–3 minutes. Pour in the coconut milk and
water, and simmer over low heat for 1 hour until the rice has
absorbed all of the liquid and the mixture has thickened.

Stir in the almonds, sugar, coconut, raisins, pistachios, and
almond slivers. Cook for a couple of minutes, stirring, until the
sugar has dissolved. Remove the pan from the heat and stir
in the ground cardamom and kewra or rosewater. Set aside to
cool, and then chill until ready to eat.

To serve, spoon into individual dishes and sprinkle with the
chopped pistachios and rose petals, if available.

We make this simple dessert regularly in the summer—loganberries, tayberries, and boysenberries also work brilliantly, as do blackberries during the wild blackberry season.

Raspberry tatin

- 3½ tablespoons butter
- scant 6 tablespoons superfine sugar
- 12 ounces raspberries (2½–3 cups)
- 2 tablespoons chopped sweet geranium leaves (*Pelargonium graveolens*)
- scant 1 cup grated Bramley apples (or other baking apple)
- softly whipped cream or crème fraîche, to serve

FOR THE CAKE
- ⅔ cup butter
- scant ¾ cup superfine sugar
- 3 large organic, free-range eggs
- 1 cup plus 2 tablespoons self-rising flour
- ¼ cup ground almonds
- zest of 1 organic lemon
- 5–6 sweet geranium leaves (*Pelargonium graveolens*)

Preheat the oven to 350°F.

Heat the butter and sugar in a 10-inch ovenproof sauté pan over low heat, stirring until melted. Simmer for 3–4 minutes, stirring frequently. Spread over the bottom of the pan and arrange the raspberries in a single layer over the top. Sprinkle with the chopped sweet geranium leaves and the grated Bramley apple.

Cream the butter and sugar until pale and creamy. Beat in the eggs, one at a time. Sift in the flour and fold into the batter. Fold in the ground almonds and lemon zest, or put everything into a food processor and whiz for 30 seconds–1 minute, just enough to combine.

Spoon the mixture over the fruit, lay 5 or 6 geranium leaves over the surface, and bake for 50 minutes. If it's browning too quickly, cover with an enamel plate or lay a piece of parchment paper on top. Let cool for 10 minutes, then turn out onto a serving plate and remove the geranium leaves if you wish.

Serve with softly whipped cream or crème fraîche.

Chocolate puddings run neck and neck with apple tarts as people's favorite dessert. My version is wickedly rich with a melting texture. It should be moist and gooey in the center, so don't overcook it or it will be disappointing and dull. This one is surprisingly good served cold.

Chocolate fudge pudding *with* toasted hazelnuts & *Frangelico cream*

- ⅔ cup unsalted butter, plus extra
  for greasing
- 5½ ounces good-quality chocolate
  (I use 52% cocoa solids)
- 1 teaspoon vanilla extract
- ½ cup plus 2 tablespoons warm water
- scant ½ cup superfine sugar
- 4 organic, free-range eggs
- 3 tablespoons self-rising flour

TO SERVE
- powdered sugar, to dust
- scant 1 cup softly whipped cream
  or crème fraîche mixed with
  1 tablespoon Frangelico
  hazelnut liqueur
- a few toasted hazelnuts,
  coarsely chopped

Preheat the oven to 400°F and grease a 1-quart pie dish with a little butter.

Chop the chocolate into small pieces and melt with the butter in a Pyrex bowl set over a pan of hot, but not simmering, water. As soon as the chocolate has melted, remove the bowl from the heat and add the vanilla extract. Stir in the warm water and sugar and mix until smooth.

Separate the eggs and whisk the yolks into the chocolate mixture. Then fold in the sifted flour, making sure there are no lumps.

In a separate bowl, whisk the egg whites until stiff peaks form, and then gently fold them into the chocolate mixture. Pour the chocolate mixture into the buttered dish.

Put the dish in a bain-marie and pour in enough boiling water to come halfway up the sides of the dish. Bake for 10 minutes. Then reduce the temperature to 315°F for a further 15–20 minutes, or until the pudding is firm on top but still soft and fudgy underneath and saucy at the base.

Set aside to cool slightly before dusting with powdered sugar. Serve warm or cold sprinkled with toasted hazelnuts with Frangelico cream or crème fraîche alongside.

SERVES 6-8

This is my original bread and butter pudding recipe, the one that people tell me over and over again is the best they've ever tasted. But there's nothing frugal about this recipe—it's got lots of plump dried fruit in it and a generous proportion of cream to milk. When people taste it, they say "Wow!" I know it has a lot of cream in it, but don't skimp—just don't eat it every day! I play around with this formula and continue to come up with more and more delicious combinations, depending on what's in season and what I have to hand (see below for some of my favorite additions). It may come as a surprise, but this bread and butter pudding reheats perfectly.

Bread & butter pudding

- 3½ tablespoons softened butter, preferably unsalted, plus extra for greasing
- 12 slices good-quality white bread, crusts removed
- ½ teaspoon freshly grated nutmeg or ground cinnamon or mixed spice (pumpkin pie spice)
- 1½ cups plump raisins or golden raisins
- 2 cups heavy cream
- 1 cup whole milk
- 4 large organic, free-range eggs, lightly beaten
- 1 teaspoon vanilla extract
- ½ cup sugar, plus 1 tablespoon for sprinkling
- a pinch of salt
- softly whipped cream, to serve

Grease a 10 x 8-inch rectangular baking dish with butter, then butter the bread. Arrange 4 slices of bread, buttered-side down, in one layer in the base of the buttered dish. It's really important to leave a generous space between each slice of bread to allow for expansion, so the pudding will be light and fluffy. Squash in too much bread and the end result will be disappointingly heavy.

Sprinkle the bread with half the freshly grated nutmeg (or cinnamon or mixed spice) and half the raisins or golden raisins. Arrange another layer of bread on top, buttered-side down, and sprinkle with the remaining spice and dried fruit. Cover with the remaining bread, buttered-side down. Leave the slices whole or cut into quarters.

In a bowl, whisk together the cream, milk, eggs, vanilla extract, sugar, and a pinch of salt. Pour the mixture through a fine-mesh strainer over the bread. Sprinkle 1 tablespoon of sugar over the top and set aside, loosely covered, at room temperature for at least 1 hour, or cover and chill overnight.

Preheat the oven to 350°F.

Put the dish in a bain-marie, and pour in enough boiling water to come halfway up the sides of the baking dish. Bake in the middle of the oven for about 1 hour or until the top is crisp and golden. Serve the pudding warm, with lots of softly whipped cream.

Variations

**BARMBRACK BREAD
& BUTTER PUDDING**

Replace the bread with barmbrack
and use mixed (pumpkin pie)
spice or cinnamon in place of
the nutmeg.

**PANETTONE BREAD
& BUTTER PUDDING**

Replace the bread with panettone.

**HOT CROSS BUN BREAD
& BUTTER PUDDING**

Replace the bread with sliced hot
cross buns (or fruit buns).

**MARMALADE BREAD
& BUTTER PUDDING**

Slather the buttered bread
generously with Seville orange
marmalade. You could also serve
some marmalade sauce as an
accompaniment, or, for an extra
treat, flavor the softly whipped
cream with Cointreau liqueur.

**CROISSANT & CHOCOLATE
BREAD & BUTTER PUDDING**

Use 4 (leftover or stale) croissants
instead of bread. Replace
the spices and raisins with
1 tablespoon of chocolate chips.

Serve this icy cold in one large dish with nougat
cookies as an extra treat or even ladyfingers.

Coffee crème brûlée

- 4 large or 5 small organic, free-range
  egg yolks
- 3 tablespoons superfine sugar
- 1½ tablespoons Camp chicory
  coffee essence
- ¾ cup plus 2 tablespoons whole milk
- ¾ cup plus 2 tablespoons heavy cream
- 8 teaspoons turbinado sugar

Preheat the oven to 300°F.

Whisk the egg yolks with the superfine sugar in a mixing bowl
until well combined. Add the coffee and whisk again. Pour in
the milk and cream and whisk gently to combine.

Pour the mixture through a nylon strainer into an 8-inch
round baking dish, approx. 1½ inches deep. Put the dish in a
bain-marie, and pour in enough boiling water to come halfway
up the side of the dish. Bake for 45–50 minutes until just set,
but still slightly wobbly in the center. Cover and chill well.

Sprinkle lightly with turbinado sugar: it should be a thin layer,
so tip off any excess if necessary. Glaze with a blow torch.
Serve chilled.

Coffee crème brulée is already very rich, but you could serve
it with a little pouring cream, if you wish, and some nougat
cookies or ladyfingers.

Make a whole dish of Tiramisu to delight your friends. The name means pick-me-up, which is not surprising considering the amount of booze it contains. Tiramisu originated in Venice, but is now served in Italian restaurants all over the world—and it always seems to taste different. I've had rave reviews for this version, which is very easy to assemble.

Tiramisu

- 2 cups strong espresso coffee
- 3 tablespoons brandy
- 3 tablespoons Jamaican rum
- 2¾ ounces bittersweet chocolate
  (I use 60% cocoa solids Valrhona)
- 3 organic, free-range eggs, separated
- 3 tablespoons superfine sugar
- 1 cup mascarpone cheese
- 38–40 ladyfingers
- unsweetened cocoa powder, to dust

Mix the coffee with the brandy and rum. Roughly grate the chocolate (I do it in the food processor with the pulse button). Whisk the egg yolks with the sugar until the mixture reaches the "ribbon" stage and is light and fluffy, then fold in the mascarpone one tablespoon at a time.

In a separate bowl, whisk the egg whites until stiff peaks form. Fold gently into the mascarpone mixture.

Now you are ready to assemble the tiramisu. Dip each side of the ladyfinger cookies, one at a time, into the coffee mixture and arrange side by side in a 10 x 8-inch dish with low sides, or a parchment-lined 8 x 4-inch loaf pan. Spread half of the mascarpone mixture gently over the cookies and sprinkle half of the grated chocolate on top. Arrange another layer of soaked cookies over the grated chocolate and spoon over the remaining mascarpone. Cover the dish with plastic wrap and set aside in the refrigerator for 3–4 hours, or preferably overnight, to allow the sponge cookies to soak up all the delicious flavors.

Just before serving, scatter the remaining chocolate over the top and dust with unsweetened cocoa powder.

If you used a loaf pan, unmold the tiramisu before serving and sprinkle with a little extra grated chocolate. Serve in thick slices with lots of whipped cream—decadent and delicious.

Tiramisu will keep for several days in the refrigerator, but make sure it is covered so that it doesn't pick up other flavors.

Variation

FROSTED TIRAMISU

Freeze the Tiramisu in a parchment-lined 8 x 4-inch loaf pan. Serve in thick slices with Irish coffee sauce. To make the sauce, put ¾ cup plus 2 tablespoons sugar and 5 tablespoons water in a heavy-based saucepan; stir until the sugar dissolves and the water comes to a boil. Remove the spoon and do not stir again until the syrup turns a pale golden caramel. Then add scant 1 cup coffee and return to the heat to dissolve to a liquid once again. Let cool and then stir in 1 tablespoon of Irish whiskey.

This is a super versatile recipe that comes from
Sue Cullinane, one of our senior tutors at Ballymaloe
Cookery School. I sometimes just scatter crunchy
praline over the top for a quick but delicious fix.
Toasted hazelnuts are also a delectable combination,
instead of the walnuts.

Sue's coffee & walnut cake

- 1 cup softened butter, plus extra
  for greasing
- scant ½ cup superfine sugar
- 6 tablespoons brown sugar
- 2¼ cups self-rising flour
- 2 teaspoons baking powder
- 4 organic, free-range eggs
- 2 tablespoons whole milk
- 1 tablespoon Camp chicory
  coffee essence

FOR THE COFFEE BUTTERCREAM
- 7 tablespoons softened butter
- 2 cups plus 2 tablespoons powdered
  sugar, sifted
- 2 teaspoons whole milk
- 2 teaspoons Camp chicory
  coffee essence
- 20 walnut halves, to decorate

Preheat the oven to 350°F. Grease a 10. x 7-inch jelly roll pan
with a little butter and line with a sheet of parchment paper
that comes up over each side.

Put all the cake ingredients into a food processor. Blend just
long enough to combine. Spread the cake mixture evenly over
the lined pan and smooth the top with a palette knife. Bake for
20–25 minutes until well risen. Remove from the oven and set
aside to cool completely in the pan.

To make the buttercream, cream the butter and beat in the
powdered sugar, followed by the milk and coffee extract.

As soon as the cake has cooled, use a palette knife to spread
the coffee buttercream evenly over the top. Cut into squares
and decorate each one with a half walnut. Alternatively, pipe
a rosette of coffee buttercream on top of each square and top
with a toasted nut.

This makes a delicious nibble to enjoy with a shot of espresso to round off a meal.

Chocolate bark *with many good things*

- 5½ ounces chocolate (approx. 62% cocoa solids)
- 1 ounce toasted hazelnuts, coarsely chopped
- 1 ounce toasted almonds, coarsely chopped
- 1 ounce pistachios, halved
- 2 ounces sour cherries or dried cranberries, halved, or plump raisins or candied orange peel, or a mixture (dried white mulberries are another delicious option)

Line a baking sheet with parchment paper.

Break the chocolate into a Pyrex bowl and sit the bowl over a saucepan of cold water. Make sure the water does not touch the bottom of the bowl. Turn on the heat under the saucepan and bring the water to a boil. Turn off the heat immediately and allow the chocolate to melt gently in the residual heat.

Pour out the chocolate onto the lined baking sheet and spread out to a thickness of ¼ inch (approx. 8 inches square). Don't worry if the edges are not even—it doesn't matter.

Sprinkle the nuts and fruit evenly over the chocolate and leave to set. Cut into rectangles or break into uneven chunks.

Serve with coffee.

Index

Acknowledgments

My 19th book and I still can't type, how feeble is that…? In fact, I should say it's *our* 19th book because Rosalie Dunne who was my PA for 24 years has typed my challenging scrawl for each and every one—so a huge thank you, yet again, to dear Rosalie—you are a total star.

My tutors here at Ballymaloe Cookery School: Tracie, Pat, Gary, Richard, Sorcha, Pam, Florrie, Shermin, and Tiffin tested and re-tested recipes with me, and I mustn't forget Tim and our farm garden team, Haulie, Eileen, Igor, David, who grow the most beautiful produce for us year round—that's what makes my simple pared-back food sing.

My current PA, Sharon Hogan, supports me in a myriad of ways to meet the deadlines.

My patient editor, Vicky Orchard, cajoles and encourages and doles out huge dollops of sage advice. Special thanks to you and to Lizzie Mayson for the beautiful photos, and of course thank you Annie Rigg for cooking my food and making it look so beautiful on the page.

Finally, to Tim and all our children and grandchildren, I love when we all sit down around the kitchen table to enjoy a bubbling pot of deliciousness together. This is what memories are made of…